The Poetry of Simon Armitage
A Study Guide for GCSE students

The Poetry of Simon Armitage

A Study Guide for GCSE students

TONY CHILDS

faber and faber

First published in 2012
by Faber and Faber Limited
Bloomsbury House
74–77 Great Russell Street
London WC1B 3DA

Typeset by Faber and Faber Ltd
Printed and bound by CPI Group (UK) Ltd, Croydon, CRO 4YY

A CIP record for this book
is available from the British Library

ISBN 978–0–571–27825–1

10 9 8 7 6 5 4 3 2 1

Contents

Foreword

I came fairly late to Simon Armitage. Somehow or other, I managed to make it through GCSEs, A levels and an English literature degree without once encountering him. Not until I was in my mid-twenties and flicking through a friend's bookcase late one evening did I come across an edition of his 1995 collection, *The Dead Sea Poems*. Caught by the title, I slid it out and began reading. Half an hour later I asked my friend if I could borrow her copy. I never gave it back.

Simon Armitage is one of the quickest, warmest, truest poets writing in the UK today. In the title poem of that first book of his that I read, the speaker – a poet – describes the poems he writes as 'everyday, effortless verse'. It's a phrase that seemed to me then, as it still does now, to sum up the easy swing of lines stuffed with run-of-the-mill phrases and characters (the difficult, dutiful family man of 'Poem'; the son who defiantly pierces his ear in 'My father thought it bloody queer') lifted directly from our daily lives.

When studying poems for exams, it's easy to think – or hard not to think – of them as codes to be cracked – safes to be broken into in order to get at the meaning locked inside. But no one who comes across 'Out of the Blue' needs to know anything about rhyme schemes to understand immediately that this is a poem about the final moments of a man who died in the Twin Towers on 9/11, just as no grounding in the finer points of syntax is required to see straight away that 'Mother, any distance greater than a single span' is talking about the necessary sadness of a son growing up and away from his mother.

In Armitage's poetry you don't need to puzzle out the meaning; it's right there in front of you. Which isn't to say his poems are shallow or simplistic. While the plain rhythms and commonplace language are instantly accessible, there's plenty lying beneath the surface, too, should you choose to mine for it. Like all great poets, Armitage's skill lies in taking those things with which we're all familiar and making them strange enough that we look at them all over again. Again, take 'Out of the Blue'. We've seen the shaky video-clip of a man waving a white shirt from a window of the blazing World Trade Center so many times now that familiarity has smoothed away a good part of the original horror. But the poem refreshes the image, and forces us to consider it anew. Finding ourselves in the position of protagonist rather than observer, we experience first hand the doomed man's terror and desperation; his baffled horror that 'others like me / should be wind-milling, wheeling, spiralling, falling'.

The great gift of poetry is to make us feel things more deeply. These poems have that gift in spades. I've been lucky enough to hear Armitage read his poems on several occasions, but the one that sticks in my mind was at a literary festival a few years back, just after he'd published his magnificent translation of *Sir Gawain and the Green Knight*. The poem, by a medieval poet whose name has long been lost, opens at Christmas, in the court of King Arthur. In the midst of the carolling and carousing, in strides a great green knight, who challenges the court to a game. One of Arthur's knights, Sir Gawain, takes up the challenge – and is plunged into a quest that leads him through the hills and forests of England and Wales, via enchantment and seduction, to a final encounter with the Green Knight in which the true meaning of his quest is revealed.

The reading took place in a tent in the middle of a field on the Welsh borders on a Novemberish day in May. The rain was lashing down, the wind had set the canvas whipping and rattling, and we were all silently counting the minutes until we could decamp for a coffee – until Armitage took to the stage. He read intently, his voice low and viscous; and his clear passion for the wild, natural poem hypnotised us almost as deeply as the words themselves. The silence in the tent was complete – and everyone forgot about their cold feet.

But wonderful as the *Gawain* poem is, it's the lines of Armitage's own poetry that I carry around in my head which have made my life richer, in small but significant ways. Every time I catch myself looking down a row of houses and mentally noting a 'dollhouse end-of-terrace / with all the trimmings', or find myself chanting 'And if it snowed and snow covered the drive . . . ' in the depths of winter, I'm grateful for them. You're reading this book now because you'll be taking an English exam in a few months' time. But in ten, twenty, fifty years, when the exam is long forgotten and you're sitting at a desk or behind the wheel of your car or pushing a trolley around a supermarket, what you'll remember, if you're lucky, are odd lines or snatches from the poems themselves. At which point I've no doubt you'll be grateful, too.

Sarah Crown, *Guardian* online literary editor

January 2012

Introduction

Simon Armitage has become one of the most popular and widely studied poets for school students, and with good reason. His writing has a very broad appeal, especially for young audiences, who enjoy the immediacy of a voice that seems to speak to them in language they understand and respond to. It's no wonder that many of the present generation identify Armitage as their 'favourite' poet, who has brought alive the study of poetry.

This book is intended to form a thorough grounding in Simon Armitage's work for students studying any of his poems for GCSE. 'Studying Poems for the Examination' invites students to explore each of the poems set for study by either OCR or AQA or Edexcel through questions around each of the Assessment Objectives that students have to address. There are also questions that take students into a wider understanding of Armitage's poetry, dealt with in the next two sections. For AQA and Edexcel there are suggestions for comparing poems within the clusters in the two anthologies.

The sections on 'Ideas and Themes' and 'Language, Structure and Form' take their titles from the Assessment Objectives. Each section is subdivided into aspects of Armitage's subjects or techniques, so that students can see the poems that they are studying in the context of all of his poetry to date, and can add to their understanding of their set poems by seeing the same ideas and techniques (or variations of them) at work in other poems.

In the 'Biography' section some of the elements of Armitage's work detailed in 'Ideas and Themes' are set in the context of his life and career to date, and questions put to him about his writing for the purposes of this book reveal some of his perceptions about his own writing.

The final section includes some sample essays written in response to actual GCSE exam questions; one at Grade C, one at A and two at A*, so that students can see what is required to achieve these grades. The strengths and weaknesses of these responses are outlined in an examiner's commentary. Whether students are studying the poems for OCR or AQA or Edexcel, the skills required for these grades are the same. For students approaching Armitage at A Level, the sections on 'Ideas and Themes' and 'Language, Structure and Form' will form a good starting point for analysing any chosen text, whether it is Homer's *Odyssey* or any of the poetry collections.

Tony Childs, 2012

Studying Poems for the Examination

In this section you can work on all of the poems by Simon Armitage which are set for study in the GCSE examinations for AQA and Edexcel. You are tested on three Assessment Objectives in the exam. More particularly:

AO1: respond to texts critically and imaginatively; select and evaluate relevant textual detail to illustrate and support interpretations

AO2: explain how language, structure and form contribute to writers' presentation of ideas, themes and settings

AO3: make comparisons between texts, evaluating writers' different ways of expressing meaning and achieving effects

Both AO1 and AO2 deal with the meanings that you can find in the poems: what you think the poems, and particular words and phrases in them, mean, and how you respond to them. The first set of questions on each poem will ask you to think about meanings, and contain suggestions about where you might look in the 'Ideas and Themes' section to help you think. Similarly, the second set of questions centres on the part of AO2 which deals specifically with the writer's methods, and how these contribute to meanings. Again, there will be suggestions about where you might look in the 'Language, Structure and Form' section to help you think about Armitage's methods in a poem or part of a poem.

In the examination you also have to compare one poem with another (AO3) in the same section of your anthology of poems. At the end of the work on each poem, you will find some suggestions about which poems you might choose for such a comparison, and the sort of features you might write about.

The GCSE poems

About His Person
Alaska
Gooseberry Season
In Our Tenth Year
Kid
'Mice and snakes don't give me the shivers'
'Mother, any distance greater than a single span'
'My father thought it bloody queer'
Poem
The Convergence of the Twain
To Poverty
True North
Wintering Out
Without Photographs
The Clown Punk
Give
A Vision
Extract from Out of the Blue
The Manhunt
Harmonium
Hitcher
'Those Bastards in their Mansions'

About His Person

Five pounds fifty in change, exactly,
a library card on its date of expiry.

A postcard, stamped,
unwritten, but franked,

A pocket-size diary slashed with a pencil
from March twenty-fourth to the first of April.

A brace of keys for a mortise lock,
an analogue watch, self-winding, stopped.

A final demand
in his own hand,

a rolled-up note of explanation
planted there like a spray carnation

but beheaded, in his fist.
A shopping list.

A giveaway photograph stashed in his wallet,
a keepsake banked in the heart of a locket.

No gold or silver,
but crowning one finger

a ring of white unweathered skin.
That was everything.

Context

'About his person' is a phrase used by police when they list the items
found on a dead person.

Meanings

1   What do the first six lines suggest to you about the personality of
    the dead man?
2   Lines 7 and 8 are about mechanisms. What do they suggest about
    the dead man?
3   Look at the last six lines. What do you learn about how the man
    feels, and what has happened to him?
4   What do you think the title of the poem means? Explore more
    than one possibility.

> → Look at the section on 'Love' in *Ideas/Themes*. How does
> the poem fit into this category? If love is being described here,
> what sort of love is it?

Language, Structure, Form

5   Count the sentences, and notice the length of each of them.
    - Why do you think there are so many short sentences? What is
      being described, or happening?
    - Why does Armitage choose to make the sentence from line 9
      to line 13 the longest one, do you think?
6   The poem is written in rhyming or half-rhyming couplets. Listen to
    the sounds that are made by the repetitions, saying them aloud or
    in your head.
    - Are the sounds generally long or short sounds? Are they hard
      or soft sounds? Why do you think Armitage has chosen these
      types of sounds for this poem?
    - Which couplet is different from the rest? Why? Think what is
      being described here.
7   The last line is 'That was everything.' This line sums up the list of
    things 'about his person'. What else might it sum up? What is the
    effect of this being the last line of the poem?

> → Look at the section on 'Summing up' in *Language,
> Structure and Form*. How does your answer to question 7 fit
> with the ways that Armitage ends other poems?

Exploring a detail

'A final demand' might suggest something about the reason for the
death. Look carefully at the sentence that begins with these words,
and decide whether it suggests:
- a financial problem
- something written to a loved one
- something written by a loved one.

It could suggest any or all of these. If you add what you have thought
about in your responses to questions 5 and 6, you will have a lot to
say about this sentence.

Alaska

So you upped
and went. Big deal!
Now you must be sitting pretty.
Now you must see me
like a big Kodiak bear,

safe and holed up
for the closed season, then rumbled.
Girl, you must see me
like the crown prince
rattling

round his icy palace,
the cook and bottle-washer gone,
snuck off, a moonlight flit
to the next estate
for sick pay, wages, running water

in their own chambers, that type
of concession. Girl,
you must picture me: clueless,
the brand of a steam iron
on my dress shirt,

the fire left on all night,
the kitchen a scrap heap
of ring-pulls and beer cans
but let me say, girl,
the only time I came within a mile

of missing you
was a rainy Wednesday, April,
hauling in the sheets,

trying to handle
that big king-sizer. Girl,

you should see yourself with him,
out in the snowfield
like nodding donkeys
or further west, you and him,
hand in hand,

his and hers,
and all this
under my nose,
like the Bering Strait,
just a stone's throw away.

Context

The Bering Strait is a 53-mile-wide channel that divides Russia and
Alaska. When you've worked through the questions below, think how
far the poem may be about the relations between Russia and the USA
in the decades after the Second World War. This period was known
as the 'Cold War' because it was a period of great tension and rivalry
between the two superpowers.

Meanings

1 After the title, the first reference (at the end of the first stanza)
   to something belonging to Alaska is 'a big Kodiak bear'. Find the
   references in the rest of the poem which might also fit with the
   title.
2 How does the speaker try to suggest that he has not been affected
   by the girl leaving him?
3 What does the speaker reveal about the male and female roles
   in the relationship that has ended? How does the speaker try to
   deny these roles? Do you believe him? Why, or why not?
4 What does the speaker's description of the girl with her new

partner in the last two stanzas reveal about how he feels and how he shows his feelings?

> → Look at the section on 'Love' in *Ideas/Themes*. How is this poem different from the other poems examined there?

Language, Structure, Form

5 'Now you must' is repeated in the first stanza. Where is the same or a similar phrase used elsewhere in the poem? Where does the phrase appear again, but changed? What does this tell you about the structure of the poem?
6 Which other word is repeated three times?
7 The new couple are described as being 'just a stone's throw away'. Why has Armitage chosen this phrase to describe how close they are, in your opinion? What does it reveal about the speaker?

> → Look at the section on 'Endings' in *Language, Structure and Form*. What sort of ending is this? How effective is the last line as an ending?

Exploring a detail

Think carefully about 'like the Bering Strait', the penultimate line of the poem.

- What does this imply about the distance between the speaker and the girl? Think about emotional distance and physical distance, and what is on each side of the Bering Strait.
- How does this relate back to the title? Is the title just a physical place or a description of a different kind of cold place?
- Say the word 'Alaska' to yourself. Apart from the name of the place, what other meaning/s can you hear?

Gooseberry Season

Which reminds me. He appeared
at noon, asking for water. He'd walked from town
after losing his job, leaving a note for his wife and his brother
and locking his dog in the coal bunker.
We made him a bed

and he slept till Monday.
A week went by and he hung up his coat.
Then a month, and not a stroke of work, a word of thanks,
A farthing of rent or a sign of him leaving.
One evening he mentioned a recipe

for smooth, seedless gooseberry sorbet
but by then I was tired of him: taking pocket money
from my boy at cards, sucking up to my wife and on his last night
sizing up my daughter. He was smoking my pipe
as we stirred his supper.

Where does the hand become the wrist?
Where does the neck become the shoulder? The watershed
and then the weight, whatever turns up and tips us over that razor's
    edge
between something and nothing, between
one and the other.

I could have told him this
but didn't bother. We ran him a bath
and held him under, dried him off and dressed him
and loaded him into the back of the pick-up.
Then we drove without headlights

to the county boundary,
dropped the tailgate, and after my boy
had been through his pockets we dragged him like a mattress

across the meadow and on the count of four
threw him over the border.

This is not general knowledge, except
in gooseberry season, which reminds me, and at the table
I have been known to raise an eyebrow, or scoop the sorbet
into five equal portions, for the hell of it.
I mention this for a good reason.

Context

Look up the meaning of the word 'gooseberry'. It's a fruit, of course, but it means something else as well, which might help you think about the relationships in the poem.

Meanings

1 What do the first three stanzas reveal about:
    - the dead man's personality
    - the speaker's personality
    - what the dead man might have done to deserve his fate, in the speaker's view?
2 The speaker describes the moment of deciding to take action as the place where the hand becomes the wrist, or the neck becomes the shoulder. Why do you think he chooses these places? What do they have in common? What might they have to do with the central action taking place in the poem?
3 What do the actions of the speaker and his family in stanzas five and six reveal about them? Think about the way their actions are described as well as the actions themselves.
4 What does the last stanza reveal about the speaker in the poem? He is only reminded of the event 'in gooseberry season'. What is revealed by what he does when he remembers the event?

> → Look at the sections on 'Crime and violence', 'Finding the words' and 'Moments' in *Ideas/Themes*. Is this an explained crime, or not? Does the speaker succeed in 'finding the words' to explain what happens? What do you make of the last line of the poem?

5   At the end of the poem the speaker talks about 'a good reason'. What 'good reason' could there be?

Language, Structure, Form

6   Why do you think the stanza describing the speaker's thoughts is exactly in the middle of the poem?

7   How is the poem structured around the phrase 'which reminds me' as a way of telling the story?

8   The death and disposal of the visitor are told very factually in stanzas five and six. What does this tell you about the speaker? The body being dragged 'like a mattress' is the only example of figurative language In the poem. What does that simile tell you about the speaker?

> → Look at the sections on 'Openings' and 'Endings' in *Language, Structure and Form*, looking for the ways that the opening and ending of this poem work.

Exploring a detail

Look carefully again at stanza four.

- The only question marks in the poem appear here. What does that tell you about the speaker's attitude in the rest of the poem?
- Stanza five begins 'I could have told him this/but didn't bother.' This appears to suggest that the thoughts in stanza four are the speaker's. Is there any evidence to suggest that

they are the poet's thoughts about moments or actions like this? What is there in this stanza which is different from the rest of the poem?

Remembering your response to question 5, you should now have plenty to write about this stanza.

In Our Tenth Year

This book, this page, this harebell laid to rest
between these sheets, these leaves, if pressed still bleeds
a watercolour of the way we were.

Those years: the fuss of such and such a day,
that disagreement and its final word,
your inventory of names and dates and times,
my infantries of tall, dark, handsome lies.

A decade on, now we astound ourselves;
still two, still twinned but doubled now with love
and for a single night apart, alone,
how sure we are, each of the other half.

This harebell holds its own. Let's give it now
In air, with light, the chance to fade, to fold.
Here, take it from my hand. Now, let it go.

Meanings

1   The relationship described in the poem is not perfect. How is this
    suggested in the words used in the first stanza?
2   How do the memories invoked in the second stanza suggest
    difficulty and conflict?
3   The third stanza suggests that, after ten years, things are much
    better now. How have things changed from the second stanza?
    Which words show this?
4   The last stanza is more complex in meaning than the first three.
    Which words suggest that the relationship is still strong, and
    which suggest that it might end? Is this is a strong relationship
    that will last, in your view? Find details from the poem to support
    your response.

→ Look at the section on 'Love' in *Ideas/Themes*. In some ways this is a very direct love poem. In what ways does it not conform to the idea of a romantic declaration of lasting love?

Language, Structure, Form

5   In the first stanza, think about 'This book'. Apart from the book that the flower is pressed in, what else might the speaker be suggesting?

6   Armitage often plays with words and the sound of words (see 'Playing with Language' in the *Language, Structure and Form* section.) How does 'This' get repeated, and changed? How does he play with the word 'inventory'?

7   The third stanza shows the relationship as it is now in numerical terms. Show how this works.

8   The last two lines of the poem have several balances of words or phrases. Find them. Why do you think Armitage makes use of these at the end of the poem?

→ The poem takes the form of a sonnet. Look at the section on 'Sonnets' in *Language, Structure and Form*. How does this poem fit into the patterns of stanza and rhyme that Armitage uses in other sonnets? Think about how the poem is structured into four stanzas, and the rhyme at the end.

Exploring a detail

The harebell could be seen as a symbol of the duration and the state of the relationship described in the poem. Work out what the first and last stanzas imply about the relationship, paying particular attention to what happens to the harebell – or what the speaker wants to happen – in the last two lines.

Kid

Batman, big shot, when you gave the order
to grow up, then let me loose to wander
leeward, freely through the wild blue yonder
as you liked to say, or ditched me, rather,
in the gutter ... well, I turned the corner.
Now I've scotched that 'he was like a father
to me' rumour, sacked it, blown the cover
on that 'he was like an elder brother'
story, let the cat out on that caper
with the married woman, how you took her
downtown on expenses in the motor.
Holy robin-redbreast-nest-egg-shocker!
Holy roll-me-over-in-the-clover,
I'm not playing ball boy any longer
Batman, now I've doffed that off-the-shoulder
Sherwood-Forest-green and scarlet number
for a pair of jeans and crew-neck jumper;
Now I'm taller, harder, stronger, older.
Batman, it makes a marvellous picture:
you without a shadow, stewing over
chicken giblets in the pressure cooker,
next to nothing in the walk-in larder,
punching the palm of your hand all winter,
you baby, now I'm the real boy wonder.

Context

Look up the meaning of the word 'batman'. Apart from it being the
name of a superhero, how might its original meaning help you think
about the relationship in the poem?

Meanings

1 What is Robin's attitude to Batman in the poem? Start from the first three words, and find any other evidence that you can.

2 What has Batman said or done to Robin to make him react in this way?

3 What relevance does the line 'he was like a father/to me' have? How was Batman 'like a father', and how might this line make you think about relationships comparable to Batman and Robin's?

4 What relationship does Robin want to put behind him? How does he see himself now?

→ Look at the section on 'Family' in *Ideas/Themes*. How is this relationship with somebody who was 'like a father' different from other family poems? This is a poem about comic-book characters, but could Robin's feelings about Batman be found in other relationships where someone is older, or in charge?

Language, Structure, Form

5 Batman and Robin are characters from a comic-book series which was then made into a television series and films, though eventually Robin was 'ditched' from the films. If you haven't seen or read any of the stories that featured Robin, look them up. Find all the ways that the actions and language of the poem echo those in the stories.

6 Work out how many sentences there are, and how long they are. How do Armitage's choices here help to capture Robin's state of mind?

7 How does the line 'Now I'm taller, harder, stronger, older' sum up how Robin feels? Notice the shape and sound of the words. How does this list fit into the overall sound and tone of the poem?

→ Look at the section 'Rants and Litanies' in *Language, Structure and Form*. How does Armitage use the words at the ends of the lines to make the poem seem like Robin ranting to Batman?

Exploring a detail

Look carefully at the last line of the poem, and write as much as you can about it. Think about:

- How 'you baby' suggests Robin's feelings about the way Batman behaves, and about their present relationship.
- Robin was known in the comics as the 'Boy Wonder'. How is he the 'boy wonder' now?
- What does the word 'real' in the last sentence imply? Think of more than one meaning.
- What relevance does the line 'he was like a father' have?

*

Mice and snakes don't give me the shivers
which I put down squarely to a decent beginning.
Upbringing, I should say, by which I mean
how me and the old man
made a good team, and never took
to stepping outside or mixing it up, aside

from the odd time when I had one word too many
for my mother, or that underwater evening
when I came home swimming
through a quart of stolen home-brewed damson wine.

So it goes. And anyway, like he says,
on the day I'm broad and bothered and bold enough
to take a swing and try and knock his grin off,

he'll be too old.

Meanings

1   The poems marked * all capture a particular voice. How do the
    first three lines of this poem show that this is the voice of a
    careful, well-balanced person? Look at the kind of words that are
    used as well as what they mean.
2   How does the speaker show his affection for his father in the poem?
3   The stanza beginning 'So it goes' appears to anticipate a future
    conflict. How does the speaker suggest that this is not a serious
    threat? Again, look at the kind of words that are used as well as
    what they mean.

> → Look at the section on 'Family' in *Ideas/Themes*. How is
> this poem similar to or different from the poems mentioned
> there about a relationship with a father?

Language, Structure, Form

4   The writing in this poem seems very simple. Why has Armitage
    chosen a simple voice for this poem? Think about your response
    to Question 1.
5   The only metaphor in the poem is in line 8, 'that underwater
    evening'. Why does Armitage use the word 'underwater' here in
    your opinion?
6   Alliteration and assonance, like rhyme, connect things together.
    Why are the words 'broad and bothered and bold' connected in
    this way, do you think?

> → The poem takes the form of a sonnet. Look at the section
> on 'Sonnets' in *Language, Structure and Form*. How does this
> poem fit into the patterns of stanza and rhyme that Armitage
> uses in other sonnets?

Exploring a detail

Armitage has made several choices about the last line of the poem.
Decide what they are, and why he has made each of the choices. You
could think about:

- the length of the line as such, and compared to the other lines
- the separation of this line from the rest of the poem
- the effect of the line as the last words of the speaker about his
  father.

*

Mother, any distance greater than a single span
requires a second pair of hands.
You come to help me measure windows, pelmets, doors,
the acres of the walls, the prairies of the floors.

You at the zero-end, me with the spool of tape, recording
length, reporting metres, centimetres back to base, then leaving
up the stairs, the line still feeding out, unreeling
years between us. Anchor. Kite.

I space-walk through the empty bedrooms, climb
the ladder to the loft, to breaking point, where something has to give;
two floors below your fingertips still pinch
the last one-hundredth of an inch . . . I reach
towards a hatch that opens on an endless sky
to fall or fly.

Context

The poem is about the moment when the young man leaves home,
and his mother comes with him to his new house to help.

Meanings

1   The speaker's mother is helping him 'measure' areas in his new
    home. As the son climbs 'up the stairs' the measuring tape is
    'unreeling/years between us'. What does this suggest about their
    relationship?
2   At the top of the ladder is the 'breaking point, where something
    has to give'. What do you think this means? Think about their
    relationship, and the measuring tape.
3   What do the last four lines say about the mother, about the son,
    and about the connection between them?

→ Look at the section on 'Family' in *Ideas/Themes*. Is the son trying to escape from his mother? Do they have a close relationship?

Language, Structure, Form

4   The poem is full of words associated with measurement. Look at any of them that you haven't thought about in your answers so far, and decide if they are about the relationship in the poem as well as just physical distance.

5   The line between the mother and the son is described as 'feeding out'. Apart from its literal meaning, what else does the word suggest in this context? You could find a similar idea in the word 'hatch' in line 13, which might suggest something else in the poem apart from just a window.

6   Look for the associations with space and sky in the third stanza. What do they suggest about the son's attitude and situation?

7   Armitage works up to the moment of decision at the end of the poem through a number of words that chime or rhyme. Look at line 10. Which sound here anticipates the last line? Now look at the words between these two sounds, and see how many times the sound in 'pinch' appears. Now look right in the middle of this pattern of sounds: find the moment of decisive action and the punctuation that clarifies it.

→ The poem takes the form of a sonnet. Look at the section on 'Sonnets' in *Language, Structure and Form*. How does this poem fit into the patterns of stanza and rhyme that Armitage uses in other sonnets? This sonnet ends on a short line, 'to fall or fly'. What is the effect of this? Think about the balance between the two words, and the space created after them.

Exploring a detail

Write as much as you can about the words 'anchor' and 'kite'. Think about:

- where they are positioned in the poem
- all the things they might imply about the mother, the son, and their relationship
- the sound of the words, and the sound of the words immediately before them
- the effect of the full stops, and the gap after the words.

*

My father thought it bloody queer,
the day I rolled home with a ring of silver in my ear
half hidden by a mop of hair. 'You've lost your head.
If that's how easily you're led
you should've had it through your nose instead.'

And even then I hadn't had the nerve to numb
the lobe with ice, then drive a needle through the skin,
then wear a safety-pin. It took a jeweller's gun
to pierce the flesh, and then a friend
to thread a sleeper in, and where it slept
the hole became a sore, became a wound, and wept.

At twenty-nine, it comes as no surprise to hear
my own voice breaking like a tear, released like water
cried from way back in the spiral of the ear. *If I were you,*
I'd take it out and leave it out next year.

Meanings

1   What does the first stanza suggest to you about the father, the
    son, and the relationship between them?
2   What does the second stanza tell you about the son?
3   'Wept' at the end of the second stanza describes what happened
    to the wound where the ear was pierced. How is the idea of
    weeping taken up and changed in the last stanza? The speaker is
    older now, and remembering. Why might he cry, do you think?

> → Look at the section on 'Family' in *Ideas/Themes*. What is
> suggested about the relationship between the son and the
> father at the time described in the first two stanzas? Do they
> have a close relationship, or not? What is the evidence for
> your answer?

Language, Structure, Form

4   The father in the first stanza seems to speak almost in clichés. How does the rhyme Armitage uses in those lines amplify this impression?

5   How do you think that the 'hole' the speaker describes in the second stanza could be seen as a hole in the relationship between father and son? Or is this a fanciful idea?

6   The poem opens with a full rhyme on the words 'queer' and 'ear'. Look at the last stanza, and see how many times the same rhyme appears (don't just look at the ends of the lines). What ideas is Armitage drawing your attention to in these words?

> → The poem takes the form of a sonnet. Look at the section on 'Sonnets' in *Language, Structure and Form*. How does this poem fit into the patterns of stanza and rhyme that Armitage uses in other sonnets? This sonnet is divided into three stanzas. Why do you think Armitage has structured the poem like this?

Exploring a detail

Concentrate on the last four lines, and write as much as you can about them. Think about:

- how water is released from the ear
- how Armitage lets the reader know that he is thinking of something a long time ago
- why you think the son's voice breaks when he repeats his father's words from years before
- why the words at the end of the poem should affect the speaker.

Add to these what you've already thought about in response to questions 3 and 6, and you'll be able to write fully about the end of the poem.

Poem

And if it snowed and snow covered the drive
he took a spade and tossed it to one side.
And always tucked his daughter up at night.
And slippered her the one time that she lied.

And every week he tipped up half his wage.
And what he didn't spend each week he saved.
And praised his wife for every meal she made.
And once, for laughing, punched her in the face.

And for his mum he hired a private nurse.
And every Sunday taxied her to church.
And he blubbed when she went from bad to worse.
And twice he lifted ten quid from her purse.

Here's how they rated him when they looked back:
sometimes he did this, sometimes he did that.

Meanings

1   What picture of the man in the poem do you get from the first
    three lines of each of the first three stanzas? Be precise rather
    than generalising.
2   What picture of the man in the poem do you get from the last line
    of each of the first three stanzas? Again, be precise rather than
    generalising.
3   Do you consider the man in the poem to be a good man, or not?
    Give reasons for your response.

> ➜ Look at the section on 'Crime and Violence' in *Ideas/
> Themes*. Is this explained violence, or not? Think about the
> last lines of all four stanzas. You could look at 'Moments', too.

Language, Structure, Form

4   There are a lot of patterns in this poem. How are the actions described in the poem balanced? Now look at the last line of the poem. How does this appear balanced on the page?

5   There is a strong rhyme scheme in this poem. Work out what it is. Then look at the vowel sounds that rhyme in the last lines of each stanza. What do you notice?

6   There is a very steady rhythm to this poem, which changes in the last stanza. How many beats are there in each line of the first three stanzas? Work it out by saying them aloud. (If you're not sure, look up what an iambic pentameter is.) Now try the same with the last two lines of the poem, and see what the difference is. Why do you think Armitage changes the rhythm for the last lines? What does it help him achieve?

7   This is a very factual poem: no imagery is used at all. In what other ways does Armitage make the poem seem so factual? Why do you think he does this?

> → The poem takes the form of a sonnet. Look at the section on 'Sonnets' in *Language, Structure and Form*. How does this poem fit into the patterns of stanza and rhyme that Armitage uses in other sonnets? You could also look at the sections on 'Lists' and 'Endings'.

Exploring a detail

Look at the first line of the poem. How does it set up how the poem works? Think about your responses to the questions above, and write as much as you can.

The Convergence of the Twain

I

Here is an architecture of air.
Where dust has cleared,
nothing stands but free sky, unlimited and sheer.

II

Smoke's dark bruise
has paled, soothed
by wind, dabbed at and eased by rain, exposing the wound.

III

Over the spoil of junk,
rescuers prod and pick,
shout into tangled holes. What answers back is aftershock.

IV

All land lines are down
Reports of mobile phones
are false. One half-excoriated Apple Mac still quotes the Dow Jones.

V

Shop windows are papered
with faces of the disappeared.
As if they might walk from the ruins – chosen, spared.

VI

With hindsight now we track
the vapour-trail of each flight-path
arcing through blue morning, like a curved thought.

VII

And in retrospect plot
the weird prospect
of a passenger-plane beading an office-block.

VIII

But long before that dawn,
with those towers drawing
in worth and name to their full height, an opposite was forming,

IX

a force
still years and miles off,
yet moving headlong forwards locked on a collision course.

X

Then time and space
contracted, so whatever distance
held those worlds apart thinned to an instant.

XI

During which, cameras framed
moments of grace,
before the furious contact wherein earth and heaven fused.

Context

This poem, which is about the destruction of the Twin Towers in New York on September 11, 2001, takes as its template a poem by Thomas Hardy, also called 'The Convergence of the Twain', which describes the sinking of the *Titanic*. It describes the sunken ship underwater, and then the formation of the iceberg, and its growth as the great ship was built, before they came together 'on paths coincident'.

Meanings

1 How does this poem work in the same way as the Thomas Hardy poem? Pinpoint the exact moment where the focus moves from the towers to the planes.
2 This poem, and the event, are more complex than Hardy's story, though. In stanza VIII, what is the 'opposite' that was forming? Opposite to what?

3   Hardy said that the collision 'jars two hemispheres'. Where in
    stanza X does the same idea emerge? What did Hardy mean, and
    what does Armitage mean?

→ Look at the section on 'Crime and Violence' in *Ideas/
Themes*. Is this explained violence, or not? Think about the
last lines of all four stanzas.

Language, Structure, Form

4   Armitage uses roman numerals to number the three line stanzas,
    as Hardy did. In Hardy's stanzas all three lines rhymed. Do these?
    Look carefully. The last stanza offers least in the way of rhymes.
    Why, do you think?
5   How does Armitage use the language and actions of injury in the
    second stanza?
6   In Stanza VI the vapour trail is described as being 'like a curved
    thought'. Why is it described in this way, in your opinion? Explore
    your reason in depth, and/or try to think of more than one.

→ Look at the section on Structure in *Language, Structure
and Form*. In what ways is this poem structured like a journey?
Look at 'endings' too. What sort of ending is this?

Exploring a detail

In Stanza VII we 'in retrospect plot' what happened. How does the
poem do this? Think about how it is structured, as well as what
happens.

To Poverty

You are near again, and have been there
or thereabouts for years. Pull up a chair.
I'd know that shadow anywhere, that silhouette
without a face, that shape. Well, be my guest.
We'll live like sidekicks – hip to hip,
like Siamese twins, joined at the pocket.

I've tried too long to see the back of you.
Last winter when you came down with the flu
I should have split, cut loose, but
let you pass the buck, the bug. Bad blood.
It's cold again; come closer to the fire, the light,
and let me make you out.

How have you hurt me, let me count the ways:
the months of Sundays
when you left me in the damp, the dark,
the red, or down and out, or out of work.
The weeks on end of bread without butter,
bed without supper.

That time I fell through Schofield's shed
and broke both legs,
and Schofield couldn't spare to split
one stick of furniture to make a splint.
Thirteen weeks I sat there till they set.
What can the poor do but wait? And wait.

How come you're struck with me? Go see the Queen,
lean on the doctor or the dean,
breathe on the major,
squeeze the mason or the manager,
go down to London, find a novelist at least

to bother with, to bleed, to leach.

On second thoughts, stay put.
A person needs to get a person close enough
to stab him in the back.
Robert Frost said that. Besides,
I'd rather keep you in the corner of my eye
than wait for you to join me side by side
at every turn, on every street, in every town.
Sit down. I said sit down.

Context

This poem is based on a nineteenth-century poem called 'An Owd Chum's Address to Poverty' by Samuel Laycock, who lived in Marsden, where Simon Armitage was born. In both poems, poverty is personified as somebody the speakers know well.

Meanings

1   In the first stanza, what clues are there that this is not a 'real' person?
2   In the second stanza, what does the speaker wish to do to Poverty? Look for more than just one thing.
3   In the third and fourth stanzas, what has Poverty done to the speaker?
4   What have all the people mentioned in stanza five got in common?
5   In the final stanza, why does the speaker want Poverty to 'stay put'?

> → Look at the section on 'Class' in *Ideas/Themes*. How does this speaker fit into the same pattern as the characters described in the section? And how not?

Language, Structure, Form

6   How does the speaker show that he wants Poverty close to him
    in the first two stanzas? Where does this idea re-emerge? Finding
    this will suggest to you the structure of the poem.
7   Armitage plays with literature in this poem. Another poet is
    referred to, apart from Laycock and Frost. Look up the phrase
    'let me count the ways' to find the answer, and then think why
    Armitage has used this reference to help define the speaker's
    relationship with Poverty.
8   Armitage plays with the sound of words to join ideas together
    in the fifth stanza. Look at the string of actions the speaker tells
    Poverty to perform, and notice the sounds of the words and
    where they are placed.

> → Look at the section on 'Playing with Language' in
> *Language, Structure and Form*. Find examples of Armitage
> playing with phrases and the sounds of words in each of the
> first three stanzas.

Exploring a detail

Look at the last three lines of the poem, and write as much as you
can about them. Think about:

- how Armitage makes both sides more insistent here by his
  choice of words
- why this is the only stanza which ends with a full rhyme
- how this completes the ideas at the beginning of the poem,
  and the beginning of the last stanza.

True North

Hitching home for the first time, the last leg
being a bummed ride in a cold guard's van
through the unmanned stations to a platform
iced with snow. It's not much to crow about,

the trip from one term at Portsmouth Poly,
all that Falklands business still to come. From there
the village looked stopped, a clutch of houses
in a toy snow-storm with the dust settled

and me ready to stir it, loaded up
with a haul of new facts, half expecting
flags or bunting, a ticker-tape welcome,
a fanfare or a civic reception.

In the Old New Inn two men sat locked
in an arm-wrestle – their one combined fist
dithered like a compass needle. Later,
after Easter, they would ask me outside

for saying Malvinas in the wrong place
at the wrong time. But that night was Christmas
and the drinks were on them. Christmas! At home
I hosted a new game: stretch a tissue

like a snare drum over a brandy glass,
put a penny on, spark up, then take turns
to dimp burning cigs through the diaphragm
before the tissue gives, the penny drops.

As the guests yawned their heads off I lectured
about wolves: how they mass on the shoreline
of Bothnia, wait for the weather, then
make the crossing when the Gulf heals over.

Context

The Falklands war occurred in the early 1980s. Argentina claimed that the islands, known in Argentina as the 'Malvinas' should belong to them, and not be a British territory.

Meanings

1   This poem could be described as a 'rite of passage' poem – it describes a moment in the speaker's transition from youth to adulthood. What indications are there in the poem that the older speaker, who tells the story, knows that he was behaving in an immature way? Why do you think he was 'ready to stir it'?

2   Why do the two older men in the pub not like the young speaker referring to the islands as the 'Malvinas'?

3   When the speaker sees his home village, travelling home 'for the first time' he thinks that it 'looked stopped'. What does he mean by this, in your opinion? Think of more than the effect of snow.

> → Look at the section on 'Journeys' in *Ideas/Themes*. The poem begins with a journey, but what other journey is being described? Don't forget there's a journey described at the end of the poem.

Language, Structure, Form

4   How does Armitage play with words and ideas in the three lines beginning 'the village looked stopped'?

5   'The Old New Inn' was a public house in Marsden. Why is its name appropriate for this poem?

6   In the last stanza, the wolves are waiting to 'make the crossing when the Gulf heals over'. Armitage uses this image to make the reader think about what has happened in the poem. What Gulf has opened up in the poem, and how will it be crossed?

➜ Look at the section on 'Metaphor' in *Language, Structure and Form*. How are the last two stanzas both built around metaphors? 'The penny drops' at the end of the sixth stanza is literal, because the penny actually drops, but the phrase means something else too. (Look up its old meaning.) How has 'the penny dropped' for the older speaker?

Exploring a detail

The combined fist of the two men arm-wrestling is described as dithering 'like a compass needle'. Write as much as you can about this moment in the poem. Think about:

- Arm-wrestling as a struggle which could go one way or the other, suggested here by the way the arms 'dithered'. What struggle is going on in the poem?
- A compass being used on a journey. How are the two men part of the compass, and the journey?
- Where is the journey pointing? Think about the title, and what it means. You might relate this to the 'Place' section in *Ideas/ Themes*.

Wintering Out

To board six months
at your mother's place, pay
precious little rent
and not lift a finger, don't think
for a minute I'm moaning.

It's a doll's house end-terrace
with all the trimmings: hanging baskets,
a double garage,
a rambling garden with
a fairy-tale ending and geese

on the river. Inside
it's odd, dovetailed into next door
with the bedrooms
back-to-back, wallpaper walls
so their phone calls ring out

loud and clear
and their footsteps on the stairs
run up and down like the practice scales
of a Grade 1 cornet lesson:
their daughter's. From day one

I've been wondering, from the morning
I hoisted the blind
and found
your mother on the lawn
in a housecoat and leggings

expertly skewering fallen fruit
with the outside tine
of the garden fork,
then casting it off, overboard

into the river. I've said

nothing, held my breath
for a whole season, waited
like Johnny Weismuller
under the ice, held on
to surface in a new house, our own

where the wood
will be treated and buffed and the grain
will circle like weather
round the knots
of high pressure. Here

we've had to button it: not fly
off the handle or stomp upstairs
yelling *That's it you bastard*
and sulk for a week
over nothing. Here

the signs are against us:
some fluke
in the spring water
turning your golden hair lime-green, honey.
Even the expert

from Yorkshire Water
taking pH tests
and far from the kettle
can't put his finger on it.
We'll have to go; leave

the bathroom with
no lock, the door that opens
of its own accord, the frostless glass
and pretty curtains
that will not meet.

It only takes one night,
your mother
having one of her moments, out
at midnight
undercoating the gutter to catch us

in the bath, fooling around
in Cinemascope. Nothing for it but to dip
beneath the bubbles,
take turns to breathe through the tube
of the loofah, sit tight

and wait for summer.

Meanings

1 At the end of the first stanza the speaker says that he's not
  'moaning'. Do you think he is? If so, how much? Is he justified, do
  you think?
2 What is the speaker's attitude to the house in the second stanza?
  Which words tell you what his attitude is?
3 What does stanza 9 suggest is wrong with living in this house? To
  what extent is this ironic?
4 What exactly is wrong with 'your mother', in the speaker's view?
  Draw your evidence from the whole poem.

> → Look at the section on 'Family' in *Ideas/Themes*. Does this
> poem fit into the ideas about family in that section, or not?

Language, Structure, Form

5 Stanzas 3 and 4 detail several things that are wrong with the
  house. How does Armitage use the sounds and meanings of words
  to move from one to another?
6 In the seventh stanza, the speaker describes himself as being

'under the ice'. What does he mean by this, in your opinion? Think of more than one reason.

7   The end of the poem details another underwater experience – in the bath. The couple 'dip/beneath the bubbles'. Apart from just hiding, what else might this suggest they have to do?

8   Look at the section on 'Endings' in *Language, Structure and Form*. How does the ending of this poem compare to others detailed there?

Exploring a detail

Look at the last line of the poem, and write as much as you can about it, asking yourself:

- what 'wait for summer' might mean
- why Armitage chooses these as the last words of the poem
- why this is the only single-line stanza.

Without Photographs

We literally stumble over the bits
and pieces, covered with ash
and tarpaulin, stashed into corners,
all that tackle under the old mill.
I don't know how we finally figure it out,
poking round in the half-dark
coming across the neatly coiled strips
of soft lead-flashing
and the fire-blackened melting equipment,
but it all fits together, falls into place.
For three weeks we light up the adapted oil-drum
with anything combustible:
door frames from the tip, spools, bobbins,
pallets, planks, old comics even which we sneak
from the house beneath our anoraks
and deliver on the run like parachute drops.

When we are forced to take a few steps backwards
and the heat stays in our faces like sunburn –
that's when the fire is hot enough.
We slide the melting-pot across the grill
 (a stewing pan with no handle, a cooking shelf)
and toss in the lumps of lead
like fat for frying with. It doesn't melt
like butter, slowly, from the bottom upwards
but reaches a point where it gives up its form
the way the sun comes
strongly around the edge of a cloud.
Then it runs, follows the dints
in the pan, covers the base so we see ourselves –
an old mirror with patches of the back missing.

For moulds we use bricks.
Like stretcher-bearers we lift the pan
between two sticks then pour the fizzing lead
into the well of a brick.
Sometimes it splits it clean in half with the heat.

Today we watch the mould, prod it
through its various stages of setting, and can't wait
to turn it out like a cake, feel
its warm weight and read the brickwork's name
cast in mirror writing along its length.
But in the days to come, the shapes will mean less
and less, giving in to the satisfaction of the work.
What there is in the sweat, and the burns,
and the blisters, is unmistakably
everlasting. Not what is struck in the forged metal
but in the trouble we know we are taking.

And something about friends, walking home,
grinning like bandits, every pocket
loaded,
all of us black-bright and stinking like kippers.

Meanings

1   In the third stanza, the speaker mentions 'the satisfaction of the work'. Find as much evidence as you can of satisfaction, either direct or implied, earlier in the poem.
2   The speaker says that the experience is 'everlasting'. Decide what he means by this – what is everlasting, and what isn't?
3   The group make bricks of lead. What else do they forge?
4   'All of us black-bright'. 'Black' and 'bright' makes an unusual combination of words. What do you think the words imply here?
5   This is a rather odd experience to enjoy. Drawing your evidence from the poem, why do you think this group enjoy it? There is

much detail suggesting that this is very hard work. Do you think this forms part of the enjoyment? Why?

6 The title of the poem is 'Without Photographs'. Why don't this group need photographs to remember the moment, in your view? Where in the poem do they see themselves?

> → Look at the sections on 'Journeys' and 'Moments' in *Ideas/Themes*. What sort of journey is this, and what sort of moment is it? What do you find the most important moment in the poem?

Language, Structure, Form

7 'The way the sun comes/strongly round the edge of a cloud'. Decide exactly why Armitage uses this idea to describe the lead changing. Think about it emotionally as well as visually.

8 Armitage mentions mirrors twice, once in the second stanza and once in the third. Why do you think he does this?

9 Why do you think the word 'loaded' is isolated as a single word line? How are the pockets 'loaded'?

> → Look at the section on 'Endings' in *Language, Structure and Form*. What sort of ending is this? What is the final effect on the reader of the poem as a whole, when the last four lines are read?

Exploring a detail

In the middle of the first stanza the speaker comments that 'it all fits together, falls into place'. Write as much as you can about the poem in the context of this line, about people and things 'fitting together'.

The Clown Punk

Driving home through the shonky side of town,
three times out of ten you'll see the town clown,
like a basket of washing that got up
and walked, towing a dog on a rope. But

don't laugh: every pixel of that man's skin
is shot through with indelible ink;
as he steps out at the traffic lights,
think what he'll look like in thirty years' time –

the deflated face and shrunken scalp
still daubed with the sad tattoos of high punk.
You kids in the back seat who wince and scream
when he slathers his daft mush on the windscreen,

remember the clown punk with his dyed brain,
then picture windscreen wipers, and let it rain.

Meanings

1   What do you learn in the poem about the appearance of the
    clown punk?
2   How do the children in the poem react to the clown punk? Why
    do you think they react in this way?
3   What is the attitude of the speaker of the poem to the clown
    punk? There may be more than one way of interpreting his
    attitude. Look for evidence of the attitude(s) right through the
    poem, not just at the end.
4   The figure described in the poem is a punk, but the title of the
    poem is 'The Clown Punk'. How is the punk like a clown? The
    other person in the poem is the speaker. How could he be like a
    clown, do you think? Could he be embarrassed by the punk? What
    would that reveal about him?

→ Look at the section on 'Outsiders' in *Ideas/Themes*. How is the clown punk made to seem like an outsider in this poem? Think about how he looks, what he does, and how other people see him.

Language, Structure, Form

5   In the first stanza, what does the writer compare the clown punk to? How does this make him seem unlike other people?
6   The writer refers to painting and colours several times in the poem. Find all the references you can. Why do you think he does this?
7   How does the writer show the effects of age on the clown punk? How is the reader invited to feel about him?

→ The poem takes the form of a sonnet. Look at the section on 'Sonnets' in *Language, Structure and Form*. How does this poem fit into the patterns of stanza and rhyme that Armitage uses in other sonnets?

Exploring a detail

Look carefully at the last line of the poem. Write as fully as you can about it, considering:

- The only full rhyme in the poem is 'brain' and 'rain' at the end. Why are these two words connected here?
- How does each word in the last line connect with the rest of the poem?
- 'Let it rain' is a command, and the last three words of the poem. Think of as many effects as you can of ending the poem with these words, and in this way.

Comparing

In the cluster 'Character and Voice', you could compare:

- The ways that attitudes to outsiders are presented in 'The Clown Punk' and 'The Hunchback in the Park'.
- The ways writers use language and form to shape the endings of 'The Clown Punk' and 'Les Grands Seigneurs'.

Give

Of all the public places, dear,
to make a scene, I've chosen here.

Of all the doorways in the world
to choose to sleep, I've chosen yours.
I'm on the street, under the stars.

For coppers I can dance or sing.
For silver – swallow swords, eat fire.
For gold – escape from locks and chains.

It's not as if I'm holding out
for frankincense or myrrh, just change.

You give me tea. That's big of you.
I'm on my knees. I beg of you.

Meanings

1 Who might the beggar be talking to? You could think of a number
   of possibilities, but give evidence for your ideas.
2 Do you think the beggar resents having to beg? Find evidence for
   your answer.
3 What might be the attitude of the other person to the beggar?
   Can you find evidence for your answer?
4 What is the beggar asking for? What is the possible significance of
   that 'dear' in the first line?

> → Look at the section on 'Outsiders' in *Ideas/Themes*. What
> defines this speaker as an outsider, do you think? When you
> are thinking about the beggar's attitude, it might be helpful to
> read the section on 'Class'.

Language, Structure, Form

5   This is a poem full of word patterns. Look carefully at the patterns
    of language in the first four lines. The final word in line 4 is 'yours'.
    What is the effect, or effects, of this word here?

6   Now look at the patterning in lines 6 to 10. Look for repetitions of
    words and sounds. How do the choices that the writer has made
    emphasise the word 'change' for the reader? Why this word? Try
    to suggest more than one reason.

> ➔ Look at the last two lines of the poem, and read the section
> in *Structure* about 'Moments that transcend, or challenge'.
> How might this be a moment of challenge?

Exploring a detail

Find as much to write as you can about the last two lines of the
poem. Think about:

- the length of the sentences, and the effects of the full stops
- the rhymes and half-rhymes, and the effects they have
- the attitudes you can find in these lines.

Comparing

In the cluster 'Character and Voice', you could compare:

- The ways outsiders are presented in 'The Clown Punk' and
  'Give'.
- The ways relationship between the speaker and another
  person are presented in 'Give' and 'The River God'.

A Vision

The future was a beautiful place, once.
Remember the full-blown balsa-wood town
on public display in the Civic Hall?
The ring-bound sketches, artists' impressions,

blueprints of smoked glass and tubular steel,
board-game suburbs, modes of transportation
like fairground rides or executive toys.
Cities like *dreams*, cantilevered by light.

And people like us at the bottle bank
next to the cycle path, or dog-walking
over tended strips of fuzzy-felt grass,
or model drivers, motoring home in

electric cars. Or after the late show –
strolling the boulevard. They were the plans
all underwritten in the neat left-hand
of architects – a true, legible script.

I pulled that future out of the north wind
at the landfill site, stamped with today's date,
riding the air with other such futures,
all unlived in and now fully extinct.

Meanings

1 In the first stanza, which words enforce the idea that this place is not real? Explain how they create this idea.
2 Now do the same for the second stanza. Why do you think the word 'dreams' is italicised?
3 Looking at the second and third stanzas, which words suggest that this is just playing, rather than a serious project?

4   Looking at the first four stanzas in full, what evidence can you find for this place being too good for ordinary people? Explain your reasons.
5   Why do you think 'other such futures' are 'all unlived in'?

> → Look at the section on 'Place' in *Ideas/Themes*. How does this place not fit into the places that Armitage usually describes?

Language, Structure, Form

6   Looking through the first four stanzas, make a list of words that suggest either the future or architects' plans.
7   Now look at the final stanza. Which words here enforce a quite different outcome to the plans? What can you say about the effect of the choice of the final word of the poem?
8   Looking through the whole poem, what words can you find which suggest toys, or things to play with? What do these choices suggest about the whole project?

> → Look at the section on 'Place' in *Ideas/Themes*. How does this place not fit into the way Armitage usually presents place?

Exploring a detail

Look carefully at the first line of the poem, and write as much as you can about it. Consider:

- How does this first line set up the whole poem? What is said about the place, and the word choices Armitage has made?
- Why does Armitage place 'once' at the end of the line instead of the beginning, in your opinion?
- Look carefully at the punctuation in this line. How does it add to the effect?

Comparing

In the cluster 'Place', you could compare:

- the ways society is presented in 'A Vision' and 'London'
- the ways the writers use the openings of 'A Vision' and 'Wind' to establish the feeling of the poems as a whole.

Extract from Out of the Blue

You have picked me out.
Through a distant shot of a building burning
you have noticed now
that a white cotton shirt is twirling, turning.

In fact I am waving, waving.
Small in the clouds, but waving, waving.
Does anyone see
a soul worth saving?

So when will you come?
Do you think you are watching, watching
a man shaking crumbs
or pegging out washing?

I am trying and trying.
The heat behind me is bullying, driving,
but the white of surrender is not yet flying.
I am not at the point of leaving, diving.

A bird goes by.
The depth is appalling. Appalling
that others like me
should be wind-milling, wheeling, spiralling, falling.

Are your eyes believing,
believing
that here in the gills
I am still breathing.

But tiring, tiring.
Sirens below are wailing, firing.
My arm is numb and my nerves are sagging.
Do you see me, my love. I am failing, flagging.

Context

This is an extract from the poem-film *Out of the Blue*, which was commissioned by Channel 5 and broadcast five years after the 9/11 attacks on America. It is told from the point of view of an English trader working in the North Tower of the World Trade Centre, and is based on a particular sequence of camcorder film taken at the time. See if you can get hold of it.

Meanings

1   The man is waving a white shirt. What different things does he imagine the onlookers might think it is?
2   As he stands in this desperate situation, what doubts and anxieties does he have?
3   The man's situation is a result of conflict. Which words show that he feels as if he is fighting now? Explain why the words you choose show this.

> → Look at the section on 'Moments' in *Ideas/Themes*. What sort of moment is this? In what ways is the man 'on the edge' at the end of the poem?

Language, Structure, Form

4   Beginning with 'building burning' in line 2, this is a poem with many repetitions or echoes of words and sounds. Go through the poem and find as many of these repetitions as you can. Hear the words in your head as you read. Why do you think Armitage chooses to do this in this poem? Think about the man's situation, and what is going on in his head.
5   In line 14 the heat is personified. What effect does this have in making the reader understand the man's feelings?
6   Look at the word 'Appalling' in line 18. What is the effect of the repetition here, and how is it heightened by Armitage in what he does with the word, and where he places it?

7   Look at the word 'believing' in line 22. It's the only one-word line
    in the poem. Why do you think this is so?

→ Look at the section on 'Playing with language' in *Language,
Structure, Form, and at 'Rants and Litanies'. How do the
features of this poem fit into the patterns described in those
sections? Count how many times Armitage uses words ending
'-ing' in the poem. What are the effects of this choice?

Exploring a detail

Look carefully at the last stanza of the poem, and write as much as
you can about it. Consider:

* Why does Armitage use short sentences in this stanza?
* Which words in the stanza suggest a sense of defeat or failure?
* 'My love' in the last line is the first mention in the poem of
  the person the speaker is addressing. What is the effect of
  mentioning her here, do you think?
* What is the effect of the last word being 'flagging', do you
  think? How does Armitage stress the word for the reader?
  Think about rhyme and punctuation.

Comparing

In the cluster 'Conflict', you could compare:

* the ways feelings are presented in 'Out of the Blue' and
  'Bayonet Charge'
* the ways the writers convey a sense of danger in 'Out of the
  Blue' and 'Belfast Confetti'.

The Manhunt

After the first phase,
after passionate nights and intimate days,

only then would he let me trace
the frozen river which ran through his face,

only then would he let me explore
the blown hinge of his lower jaw,

and handle and hold
the damaged, porcelain collar-bone,

and mind and attend
the fractured rudder of shoulder-blade,

and finger and thumb
the parachute silk of his punctured lung.

Only then could I bind the struts
and climb the rungs of his broken ribs,

and feel the hurt
of his grazed heart.

Skirting along,
only then could I picture the scan,

the foetus of metal beneath his chest
where the bullet had finally come to rest.

Then I widened the search
traced the scarring back to its source

to a sweating, unexploded mine
buried deep in his mind, around which

every nerve in his body had tightened and closed.
Then, and only then, did I come close.

Context

This poem is taken from 'The Not Dead', a short collection of war poems written, not in battle, but as a response to the testimonies of ex-soldiers featured in a Channel 4 documentary of the same name, broadcast on Remembrance Day 2007. As Simon Armitage pointed out in his introduction, time is no 'great healer' for people scarred by war. This is the story of the wife of a soldier who had been shot by a bullet which ricocheted round his body, and her struggle to mend the emotional as well as the physical scars.

Meanings

1   The poem is about a bullet ricocheting around a soldier's body after he has been shot. Trace the course of the bullet through the poem.
2   Pick out all the words which say, or imply, damage, and all the words which suggest help or healing.
3   At the end of the poem the speaker says that 'only then, did I come close'. What does she 'come close' to, do you think? It might help to think about the last part of the man's body that she mentions.

> → Look at the section on 'Journeys' in *Ideas/Themes*. How is this poem like a journey? Which poems mentioned in the 'Journeys' section might it be like?

Language, Structure, Form

4   Trace all the repetitions of 'and' and 'only then'.
    • How do they add to the sense of a journey?
    • Where does the last repetition of 'and' appear? Why here, do you think?
5   Each body part identified in the poem, except the heart, is described using a metaphor. Find them all, and consider the effect of each one.

6 Why do you think Armitage does not use a metaphor to describe the heart? How else are the lines describing the heart different from the rest of the poem?

7 The bullet itself is described as a 'foetus of metal'. Why, do you think?

> → Look at the sections on 'Metaphor' in Language and 'Different shapes and forms' in *Form*. How has Armitage used metaphors in the poem as a whole? How does the use of couplets help the design of the poem's story?

Exploring a detail

Look carefully at the line 'the parachute silk of his punctured lung', and write as much as you can about it. Think about:

- what each word implies or suggests. Think of as many things as you can
- the effect of the sounds repeated in the last two words.

Comparing

In the cluster 'Relationships', you could compare:

- the ways damage to somebody is presented in 'The Manhunt' and 'Quickdraw'
- the ways the writers use language to present a relationship in 'The Manhunt' and' Quickdraw'.

Harmonium

The *Farrand Chapelette* was gathering dust
in the shadowy porch of Marsden Church,
and was due to be bundled off to the skip.
Or was mine for a song, if I wanted it.

Sunlight, through stained glass, which on bright days
might beatify saints or raise the dead,
had aged the harmonium's softwood case
and yellowed the fingernails of its keys.
And one of its notes had lost its tongue,
and holes were worn in both the treadles
where the organist's feet, in grey, woollen socks
and leather-soled shoes, had pedalled and pedalled.

But its hummed harmonics still struck a chord:
for a hundred years that organ had stood
by the choristers' stalls, where father and son,
each in their time, had opened their throats,
and gilded finches – like high notes – had streamed out.

Through his own blue cloud of tobacco smog,
with smoker's fingers and dottled thumbs,
he comes to help me cart it away.
And we carry it flat, laid on its back.
And he, being him, can't help but say
that the next box I'll shoulder through this nave
will bear the freight of his own dead weight.
And I, being me, then mouth in reply
some shallow or sorry phrase or word
too starved of breath to make itself heard.

Context

A 'Farrand Chapelette' was a brand of harmonium – a foot-pumped keyboard instrument similar to a reed organ, very popular at one time in small chapels and churches. Both Armitage and his father had been involved with the church, and when the old harmonium in Marsden church was being replaced Simon bought it.

Meanings

1 In the poem the writer compares the harmonium to his father. Starting with 'gathering dust' in the first line, look through the poem for all the references you can find to things which are ageing, disappeared, or about to be disposed of. Which of these might be like the father, and how?

2 The speaker says in line 13 that the old harmonium 'still struck a chord' with him. Why do you think the instrument appeals to him?

3 The father and son 'carry it flat, laid on its back'. How does this idea connect with the last five lines of the poem?

4 In the last six lines of the poem, what is revealed about the character of the two people? What is the son's attitude to the father?

> → Look at the section on 'Family' in *Ideas/Themes*. In the whole poem, what is revealed about the father and the son, and their relationship?

Language, Structure, Form

5 How is the harmonium personified in lines 7–9?

6 Look for all the references to music and singing in the poem, and what sort of musical sounds are being described. The title of the poem is 'Harmonium'. How do these things connect with the relationship between the father and the son?

7 'Will bear the freight of his own dead weight'. How does the

rhyme in this line, and the full stop at the end, add to the effect of what is being described?

> → Look at the sections on 'Finding the Words' in *Ideas/Themes* and 'Balancing' in *Endings*. Now look carefully at the last six lines of the poem, thinking about all the balances you can find between the father and son, and how they are described.

Exploring a detail

Examine the way that breath and air are used throughout the poem. Think about:
- how a harmonium works
- the references to singing and songs
- anything else you can find.

Why do you think the poem ends in silence, with no breath?

Comparing

In the cluster 'Relationships', you could compare:
- The ways feelings about parents are presented in 'Harmonium' and 'Praise Song for my Mother'.
- The feelings about a family member shown in 'Harmonium' and 'My Sister Maude'.

Hitcher

I'd been tired, under
the weather, but the ansaphone kept screaming:
One more sick-note, mister, and you're finished. Fired.
I thumbed a lift to where the car was parked.
A Vauxhall Astra. It was hired.

I picked him up in Leeds.
He was following the sun to west from east
with just a toothbrush and the good earth for a bed. The truth,
he said, was blowin' in the wind,
or round the next bend.

I let him have it
on the top road out of Harrogate – once
with the head, then six times with the krooklok
in the face – and didn't even swerve.
I dropped it into third

and leant across
to let him out, and saw him in the mirror
bouncing off the kerb, then disappearing down the verge.
We were the same age, give or take a week.
He'd said he liked the breeze

to run its fingers
through his hair. It was twelve noon.
The outlook for the day was moderate to fair.
Stitch that, I remember thinking,
you can walk from there.

Meanings

1   What do you learn in the first stanza about the speaker's situation

and mood? Find as many reasons as you can in this stanza for the man behaving in the way that he does.

2   From the information in the second stanza, what sort of character does the hitcher seem to be? How is he different from the speaker of the poem?

3   What more is revealed about the speaker in the rest of the poem? Look at the last stanza as well as the action in the middle of the poem.

4   What is the attitude of the speaker to the hitcher? Why do you think he attacks him? What clues can you find about the speaker's personality which might explain his actions?

> → Look at the section on 'Crime and Violence' in *Ideas/Themes*. Is this explained violence, or not? How far is it explained, or not? You could look at 'Moments', too, to help you think about the nature of this poem.

Language, Structure, Form

5   There are several short, simple sentences in the poem. Choose two, and decide why Armitage has used these short sentences. Might they reveal something about the speaker's attitude or personality?

6   How does the act of violence in the poem seem to you – cold, vicious, detached, or something else? What language has Armitage used to make you react in the way you did?

7   How is the onset of violence made to seem sudden?

8   There are five sentences in the last seven lines. What does this tell you about the character of the speaker? Remember what has happened before this moment.

> → Look at the section on 'Endings' in *Language, Structure and Form*. What sort of ending is this? What effect do the last two lines have on the reader?

→ Look at the 'Different shapes and forms' section in *Form*. Work out the stanza pattern. Although some sentences are short, others flow across line breaks and even stanza breaks. Choose two of these, and decide why you think Armitage has done this. Do they say something about an action or a character?

Exploring a detail

'We were the same age, give or take a week'. Write as much as you can about this line. Think about:

- why Armitage includes this information for the reader
- why he places it exactly where he does
- how the speaker would know that 'we were the same age, give or take a week'? Perhaps there is a hint here that this might be two sides of the same person. Read the 'Biography' section to find a suggestion about how this might be correct. What evidence can you find in the poem to support this view?
- If you conclude that the two characters in the poem are two sides of the same person, what might the conflict in the poem be about?

Comparing

In the cluster 'Clashes and Collisions', you could compare:

- how 'Hitcher' and 'Invasion' show acts of violence
- how 'Hitcher' and 'Catrin' present feelings.

*

Those bastards in their mansions:
to hear them shriek you'd think
I'd poisoned the dogs and vaulted the ditches,
crossed the lawn in stocking feet and threadbare britches,
forced the door of one of the porches, and lifted
the gift of fire from the burning torches,

then given heat and light to streets and houses,
told the people how to ditch their cuffs and shackles,
armed them with the iron from their wrists and ankles.

Those lords and ladies in their palaces and castles,
they'd have me sniffed out by their beagles,
picked at by their eagles, pinned down, grilled
beneath the sun.

Me, I stick to the shadows, carry a gun.

Context

The Greek hero, Prometheus, is in the background of this poem.
Prometheus stole fire from the gods to give to men. His punishment
was to be chained to a rock and have his liver pecked out each day by
an eagle. He is often seen as a symbolic figure of revolt against cruelty
and tyranny.

Meanings

1   What do the 'lords and ladies' have that the speaker hasn't? What is
    his attitude to them? Look for more than the first line as evidence.
2   What is the attitude of the 'lords and ladies' to the speaker, and,
    according to him, to the people in 'streets and houses'?
3   How is the speaker like the hero Prometheus, and how isn't
    he? What do you think the last line implies about him? Suggest
    more than one way of interpreting the line.

→ Look at the section on 'Class' in *Ideas/Themes*. How does this poem fit into attitudes to class? How does Armitage make the reader sympathise with the speaker's side? Sometimes Armitage deliberately mocks Northern stereotypes. Do you think he is doing that here?

Language, Structure, Form

4   Armitage uses sounds to capture the speaker's voice in the first stanza. Count the number of 'd', 't' and 's' sounds, and decide why Armitage has used these so frequently.

5   In lines 3 to 9, pick out the verbs that describe the speaker's actions. What do they tell you about the speaker? Notice where the verbs fall in the lines. What is the effect of this choice, in your view?

6   Now pick out the verbs in lines 11 and 12 that describe what the 'lords and ladies' might do. What do these words tell you about them? When you put them together, how do they sound similar?

→ Look at the 'Sonnets' section in *Form*. Work out the stanza pattern, and look for the rhymes and half-rhymes. How is each stanza about something different?

Exploring a detail

Write as much as you can about the last line of the poem. Consider:
- what it says about the speaker and his situation, and his view of himself
- the word order, the punctuation and the verbs
- why this line is a single line at the end
- why the poem ends on the word that it does, and how Armitage draws the reader's attention to this word
- how you view the speaker at the end of the poem. What is he?

Comparing

In the cluster 'Taking a Stand', you could compare:

- how 'Those bastards in their mansions' and 'The Penelopes of my homeland' show the victims of oppression
- the methods the writers use to present man in 'Those bastards in their mansions' and 'On the Life of Man'.

Aspects of Simon Armitage's Poetry

This section gives an overview of Simon Armitage's work, divided into sections which follow the GCSE Assessment Objectives. These are:

Ideas and Themes

Outsiders
Class
Crime and violence
Love
The Body
Family
Finding the Words
Moments
Journeys
Place
Time

Language, Structure and Form

Language
The language of the North
Playing with language
Metaphor

Structure
Openings
Lists
Journeys
Endings
Summing up
Balancing
Moments that transcend, or change

Form
Different shapes/forms
Sonnets
Rants and litanies

Ideas and themes

This section examines some of the ideas and themes that occur throughout Simon Armitage's work.

Outsiders

'the shonky side of town' (*The Clown Punk*)

Figures who belong to an underclass in society occur frequently in Armitage's work. They are marked out by appearance and behaviour. The figure in 'The Clown Punk', with his 'sad tattoos' looks like 'a basket of washing', while the beggar in 'Give' is literally on the outside, in a doorway. The boy in 'A Painted Bird for Thomas Szasz' has 'foam lining hanging from a split seam' and 'smelt like a wet dog, drying', spends his time 'pretending to direct the buses' and is seen 'pissing himself through his pants'. The people are often placed at the margins, in 'the shonky side of town' ('The Clown Punk'), the 'Probation Day Centre' ('A Painted Bird for Thomas Szasz') or simply in 'the shadows' ('Those Bastards in their Mansions').

The effect of these figures is striking: these are not simply descriptions. The feelings they produce are sometimes given directly ('He bothered me' in 'A Painted Bird for Thomas Szasz'), and sometimes figuratively ('The dark circle of his stain' in 'A Painted Bird' was 'still growing outward slowly, like a town' as though the boy himself is a stain).

Perhaps Armitage gets closest to describing his very personal feelings for the damaged or disadvantaged members of society in the last verse of 'It Ain't What You Do It's What It Does To You'.

> And I guess that the tightness in the throat
> and the tiny cascading sensation
> somewhere inside us are both part of that
> sense of something else. That feeling, I mean.

This 'what it does to you' is difficult to define exactly, but it has clearly to do with the emotions of the person involved, and also appeals to individuals in society as a whole ('us') and perhaps reflects a larger agenda in 'that sense of something else'. Even in *Sir Gawain and the Green Knight*, Gawain, who is hardly an outsider, has to pass 'long dark nights unloved and alone'. Perhaps this is one of the reasons that Armitage was drawn to his story.

See also (AQA):
'Horse Whisperer' (Andrew Forster)
'The Hunchback in the Park' (Dylan Thomas)
'At the Border, 1979' (Choman Hardi)

Class

The speaker in 'Those bastards in their mansions', with his 'stocking feet and threadbare britches', while clearly comparable to the underclass figures mentioned above, is also very different. This is a figure well aware of class differences, and resentful of privilege. Others are presented more neutrally. The 'Goalkeeper with a Cigarette' is 'a man who stubs his reefers on the post', who 'is what he is, does whatever suits him', outside conventional behaviour or morality.

Often, however, there is a very clear line drawn between classes. 'The Laughing Stock' creates a deliberately stereotyped view of working-class behaviour, contrasted sharply with 'friends of the Queen' and encapsulated in the line 'We're watching a show: *How the Other Half Live*.' There is a border between 'us' and 'the other half': 'One of us scrubs up well, crosses/the border', but is found out. Although the division appears sharp, and difficult to breach, Armitage seems insistent that it is nurture, not nature, which forms the barrier. In 'The Two of Us' two figures on the same land stare at each other across the class divide.

> You sat sitting in your country seat
>
> and
>
> me darning socks, me lodging at the gate

seem different in possessions, attitudes, and how they are perceived, but at the same time 'Some in the village reckon we're alike, akin'. The final line seems like a warning as well as an insistence on the equality of death: 'the worm won't know your make of bone from mine.' In these first-person narratives, it is noticeable that the speaker always belongs to the 'lower' of the two classes, suggesting that this is where the writer's sympathies lie. The one exception might be in 'Hitcher', but even here the speaker notes that 'We were the same age, give or take a week' – two sides of the same coin again, possibly.

See also (AQA):
'The Ruined Maid' (Thomas Hardy)
'Hard Water' (Jean Sprackland)
'At the Border, 1979' (Choman Hardi)

Crime and Violence

'I have lived with thieves in Manchester' (*It Ain't What You Do It's What It Does To You*)

Given Armitage's early employment as a probation officer, it is no surprise that themes of crime and violence are present in his first collection, *Zoom!*, and continue to surface in his writing. The peripheral figures mentioned above are often on the edges of crime, perhaps only as observers, such as the speaker in 'Man on the Line', who finds a suicide victim and knows that 'creeps like me spray-painting the carriages' are part of a 'strange crowd'. So too is the watcher in 'On Miles Platting Station', itself a damaged environment, with a vista of 'near-derelict buildings' and 'a broken cable'. The vegetation is 'stitchwort' – the name suggesting damage in itself – and the police have found 'new evidence' hidden behind a windbreak. Although the reader does not know what the crime is, the mention of Saddleworth Moor associates it with the Brady and Hindley murders.

An observer who is also an actor in the crime scene is the 'Boy out-side the Fire Station', who hangs around observing the fire engines and firemen because 'I just like watching', but he's 'up to something' with his petrol and matches. The pickpocket in the football crowds in 'Brassneck' is a straightforward criminal, but, as in 'Hitcher', there's also a hint of a class divide: the speaker's friend Carter thinks 'my voice a little too tongued and grooved'. In 'Angoisse' a crime is con-sidered, but not carried out. With a glance at Camus, an act of sense-less violence is not committed, whereas in 'Hitcher' it is. In 'Goose-berry Season' murder is presented coldly, without an explanation:

> I could have told him this
> but didn't bother. We ran him a bath
> and held him under

Two poems in a short sequence of poems, 'Sympathy', look at the effects of crime, in the voices of the victims. Other Armitage char-acteristics appear here: one of the criminals, an acquitted murderer, is a peripheral figure in society, but not presented sympathetically:

> You know t'sort:
> Mettallica T-shirt, trainers, camouflage shorts,
> number-four cropped curly 'air and pony-tail,
> tatts on 'is forearms.

Class is an issue in the case of the hit-and-run death at the hands of the driver of the 'soft-top Merc with the roof rolled down'.

Casual violence (or at least apparently casual violence) appears several times. In 'Gooseberry Season' and 'Hitcher' violence appears suddenly, with no warning to the reader ('We ran him a bath/and held him under' in 'Gooseberry Season' and 'I let him have it' in 'Hitcher'). Both these acts have some sort of reason behind them, unlike 'And once, for laughing, punched her in the face' in 'Poem'. A feature of *Sir Gawain and the Green Knight* is the violent nature of much of the action, not only in the central conflicts but in the descriptions of the butchery of the various animals hunted and slaughtered:

> The cleanness of the strike cleaved the spinal cord
> and parted the fat and the flesh

More complex, and more disturbing, is the violent self-harm shown in 'I say I say I say' ('Anyone opened their wrists/with a blade in the bath?'). The grim nature of the cutting is made more disturbing by being presented in the language of stand-up comedy, signalled by the title and the first line, 'Anyone heard the one about . . .', and with the voice conjuring up an audience ('Those in the dark at the back', and 'Those in the front in the know'). It is no less disturbing to see self-harm presented in the context of entertainment, as in a television programme with an audience. At the same time, the violence is more complex than the simple acts in the previous poems because of the healing possibility of 'a little love' offered at the end; there is no love apparent in 'Hitcher 'or 'Gooseberry Season'.

The graphic violence in 'I say I say I say' is found again in 'A Week and a Fortnight'. The balance between love and hurt is here, in the religious context of 'the seven acts of mercy and the fourteen stations of the cross'. Although the life is 'saved at the last', there is nevertheless twice as much suffering in the fourteen stations than in the seven acts. Images of torture and damage run through the poem, about a life 'marked with the cross in the eye of a rifle'. The phrase contains the religious image of the cross but translates it into a modern kind of threat, shown later in 'bunged with a bottle of petrol and bleach' and 'dabbed on the foot with a soldering iron'. The same desperate, unloved life as in 'I say I say I say' is suggested by 'Left for an hour with booze and a razor', though here too 'a little love' appears when the life is 'carted by ambulance clear of the woods'. Essentially, though, the poem pictures 'life for the lost': more shadowy figures at the edges of society.

See also (AQA):
'The River God' (Stevie Smith)
All of the poems in 'Conflict'
Nettles (Vernon Scannell)

Love

'I was still learning to drive' (*Missed It by That Much*)

Armitage's early poems tend, understandably, to deal with young love, and often obliquely rather than directly. A rare example of being direct is:

> that was just my butterfingered way, at thirteen,
> of asking you if you would marry me. (*I am very bothered
>   when I think . . .*)

More often, emotion is conveyed through symbolism and imagery, as in 'Map Reference', where the loved one is compared to the mountain which 'stood where it stood, so absolutely, for you'. The mountain is fixed, a point of certainty, reflecting the way that the male speakers in these poems seem unsure and the females sure. In 'Missed It by That Much', another poem of early love, the ending reflects the same tendency to suggest through imagery, and the same difference in confidence:

> I think you kept the map.
> I was still learning to drive.

In 'Girl', the male speaker expresses his attraction through the orange that has been dropped into his satchel, 'happy/with the extra weight', and can't think what to do except pass by the stall on 'no particular errand'.

'Potassium' is another poem of love at an early age, indicated by 'her anxious sister was coming, ready or not.' It begins with a clearly stated moment of physical contact:

> and let the soft, red
> bubble of her mouth break
>
> gently into my own.

The poem then works through images of focus ('a bull's eye'), explosions (a 'firework') and the onset of passion ('the roar of the engines'), before ending with a clear suggestion of the movement to adult life:

> Through
> the fog the mainland
> was always
> just beginning.

Later poems become more explicit, but often deal with damage rather than the uncertainty or shyness of youth. 'An Accommodation' depicts a husband and wife who have formed a permanent truce in their conflict by hanging a net curtain between them, dividing their space in two. 'The Manhunt' is in the voice of the wife of an injured soldier, who is tracing the path of the bullet that ricocheted through him. When she finds the hurt buried 'deep in his mind' she can finally 'come close'. This is similar in a way to 'I've made out a will', where the end of the list of body parts is

> the pendulum, the ticker;
> leave that where it stops or hangs.

A direct statement of love appears in the last poem in the sequence, 'Reading the Banns'. If the speaker's wife were to 'Lay/your sleeping head' on his arm (with a glance at W. H. Auden's poem of the same title), then

> I should rather
> cleave it from the joint or seam
>
> than make a scene
> or bring you round.

Even here, Armitage cannot quite leave it at such a bald declaration, but typically ends on a note which produces some irony, or distance, or uncertainty:

> There,
> how does that sound?

A later poem, 'In Our Tenth Year' is much more reflective, looking back on 'the way we were' and concluding that the couple are

> Still two, still twinned, but doubled now with love.

See also (AQA):
'Medusa' (Carol Ann Duffy)
'Singh Song' (Daljit Nagra)
'Brendon Gallacher' (Jackie Kay)
All of the poems in 'Relationships'

The Body

'the web of nerves and veins, the loaf of brains' ('I've made out a will')

As in 'The Manhunt', much of Armitage's writing about the human body centres on damage. 'For the Record' takes an essentially comic view of a tooth extraction, but 'ankylosing spondylitis' offers only desperation. The machinery of the body,

> the clockwork of my joints and discs,
> the ratchet of my hips

is 'fossilising' and fragile, 'like glass, like ice'. The isolated last line

> Don't leave me be. Don't let me sleep

is a desperate plea.

The machine imagery in 'ankylosing spondylitis' becomes literal in 'The Winner', an essentially comic view of body parts being replaced by metallic. The speaker here has 'his nerves of steel and his iron will', and the poem ends with the heart, with a change to an ironic mood.

> a heart
> like a water-pump under a battleship chest

could be seen as ironic, or celebratory, or both.

'I've made out a will' also dwells on the contents of the body – 'the jellies and tubes and syrups and glues' in lighthearted imagery, 'blood – a gallon exactly of bilberry soup'. The grandfather clock images culminate in the heart again, but the heart here surviving, suggesting some sort of hope, unlike the bleak picture at the end of 'ankylosing spondylitis'.

See also (AQA):
'Casehistory: Alison (head injury)'
(U. A. Fanthorpe)

Family

'Oh Ma/treasure this badge that belongs to your son'
   (*The Winner*)

Armitage reveals his thoughts about his family in a few deeply felt poems. In 'Mother any distance greater than a single span' the mother seems to be clinging on to the 'last one hundredth of an inch' of her relationship with her son. He is ready to 'fly' from the nest, as the space imagery in the final stanza leads to the perception of 'the endless sky' above him. 'Anchor. Kite' in the centre of the poem is an ambivalent image, but the reader can't escape feeling that she will always be 'a second pair of hands' for him, ready to catch him should he 'fall', and he knows this. A much less complex transition is shown in 'The Straight and Narrow', where the schoolboys catch a glimpse of a working life ahead, with the writer again employing space imagery to show it:

> The clouds opened up; we were leaving the past,
>   drawn by a star that had risen inside us.

The father, like the mother in 'Mother any distance', is recalled by an older narrator in 'Greenhouse'. Remembering working with his father in the construction of the greenhouse, the speaker also remembers seeing his father come home at night, and his feeling of kinship is established as he sees,

> caught in the blur of double glazing
> your perfect ghost, just one step behind you.

The son here seems glad to be following in his father's footsteps. At first the father in 'My father thought it bloody queer' seems a stern figure, lacking the mother's warmth suggested in 'Mother any distance', but the older narrator, looking back on the incident of the earring, finds his voice 'breaking like a tear', suggesting a feeling for his father which is 'no surprise' to him, though he doesn't quite articulate what it is.

Ending with this sort of moment is a pattern that recurs in 'Harmonium'.

> And I, being me, mouth in reply
> some shallow or sorry phrase or word
> too starved of breath to make itself heard.

The three early poems mentioned above deal with rites of passage as the young man moves towards adult independence. In this much later poem, a different transition is touched on, as the son is forced by his father's words to think about the reality of a parent's death.

See also (AQA):
'On a Portrait of a Deaf Man' (John Betjeman)
'The Blackbird of Glanmore' (Seamus Heaney)
'Poppies' (Jane Weir)
'Brothers' (Andrew Forster)
'Praise Song for my Mother' (Grace Nichols)
'Sister Maude' (Christina Georgina Rossetti)
'Nettles' (Vernon Scannell)
'Born Yesterday' (Philip Larkin)

Finding the Words

'That feeling, I mean' (*It Ain't What You Do It's What It Does To You*)

A recurring idea in Armitage's poetry from his earliest published work has been the difficulty of finding the words to express emotions. This is often shown through the use of familiar words and phrases, to illustrate how elusive more exact expressions are. The final stanza of 'It Ain't What You Do It's What It Does To You' is interesting in this respect. Armitage starts by trying to express exactly what the feelings are, though he's not sure that he's got it right:

> And I guess that the tightness in the throat
> and the tiny cascading sensation
> somewhere inside us

and then resorts to words which he knows the reader will recognise as vague:

> are both part of that
> sense of something else. That feeling, I mean.

Sometimes the exact words can't be spoken because of the strength of emotion, as in 'Harmonium', above. Equally, the lack of words sometimes shows a failure to speak, perhaps revealing a reluctance to admit to or articulate emotion, as in 'To His Lost Lover':

> And left unsaid some things he should have spoken,
> about the heart, where it hurt exactly, and how often.

These words read as failure, even tragedy, where for the young it might be presented as comedy. In 'I am very bothered when I think' the boy sees the ring heated in the Bunsen burner as his 'butter-fingered way' of asking the girl to marry him – without words, that is.

All of the examples above form the endings of poems, as did some in the last section about emotions, suggesting here that this is no marginal problem in the poems: it's where they are leading. The same can be true when an action rather than an emotion is being explained. It's hard to do it. In 'Poem', for instance, the man's contradictory actions are explained (or rather not) in the last line:

> sometimes he did this, sometimes he did that.

'Gooseberry Season' deals with the decision to take an action, the 'watershed' between thinking something and doing it, and again the poet can't find the words to describe the moment:

> that razor's edge
> between something and nothing, between

one and the other.

The poem ends with a further reluctance to explain, dressed up in a common phrase:

> I mention this for a good reason.

Perhaps, though, this lack of words isn't a failure at all, but what the writer prefers, as he comments in one of the 'Book of Matches' poems:

> That's
> when I like love best – not locked away
> but left unsung, unsaid.

See also (AQA):
'The Right Word' (Imtiaz Dharker)

Moments

'Then distant thoughts were suddenly blindingly clear' (*The Wood for the Trees*)

Armitage is often drawn to examine dramatic moments or moments of revelation. The end of 'Not the Furniture Game' displays both. After 44 lines describing 'he' in various ways, most of them implying size and strength, two lines describe 'she' as 'a chair, tipped over backwards'. The moment of shock robs the man of all that has built up, and his implosion is described in the last lines in a striking, dramatic image:

> his face was a hole
> where the ice had not been thick enough to hold her.

The poem is partly a psychological study of the man in the poem, and his relationship with the woman, though this only emerges at the end. The same is true of the strange narrative in 'I'll Be There to Love and Comfort You'. The startling moment at the end, hinted at earlier in 'she'd be twenty-four by now', is again expressed in a transforming image, of

> the pulsing starfish of a child's hand, swimming and swimming and coming to settle on my upturned palm.

A first-person psychological study of paranoia, 'The Stake-Out', ends in a moment suggesting a dramatic resolution:

> The moment they see me, I'll shoot.

A less dramatic state of paranoia is explored in 'Working from Home', but the resolution is similar, as the speaker imagines the tree-cutter's

> lips in the letterbox, wanting to speak.

Other poems are built around examining the effects of situations of drama or conflict, such as the appearance of the horses in 'Horses, M62' or the burnt finger in 'I am very bothered when I think'.

See also (AQA):
'The Moment' (Margaret Atwood)
'Cold Knap Lake' (Gillian Clarke)
'Crossing the Loch' (Kathleen Jamie)
Extract from 'The Prelude' (William Wordsworth)
'Spell bound' (Emily Jane Bronte)
'The Right Word' (Imtiaz Dharker)
'At the Border, 1979' (Choman Hardi)
'Bayonet Charge' (Ted Hughes)

Journeys

'I wondered/about home, the long journey backwards' ('The Wood for the Trees')

Armitage's poetry is full of journeys of different types. The title poem of his first collection, 'Zoom!', appears to be simply a physical journey, matching the child's address which ends 'the universe'. 'It begins as a house . . . but it will not stop there', as it zooms further and further into space. In the end it is revealed as a journey of the imagination, 'just words'. 'The Tyre' is a similar journey – a physical one, as the tyre is pushed down the hill and gets 'carried away with its own momentum'. A moment of transformation occurs again, though. When the tyre cannot be found, and has left no trace, it's as if it had

> at that moment gone beyond itself
> towards some other sphere, and disappeared.

Another physical journey is suggested by 'the road over the knoll' in 'Butterflies'. It's 'a stepping off into the unknown', with the poet recognising the urge to travel:

> some instinct in the toes or heel
> wants to let rip over the brow of that hill.

As with most of Armitage's subjects, journeys can also be treated comically. 'Ten Pence Story' follows the journey of a coin from coming 'out of the melting point, into the mint'. The title of 'An Expedition' suggests a journey, and is expressed in the language of travel, in the repeated phrase 'we pushed on through' and in verbs such as 'traversed', 'bivouacked', and 'descended'. The poem actually describes a journey into the elements of a house, however, beginning on the surface with the 'Great Artex Shield' and the 'Plains of Anaglypta' and working inwards. The ending takes on a more serious note, as

> Each heart went on. Where else to head for
> but the fixed eventuality of earth, water or stone.

The answer to 'where else' is revealed in the last line, in which the repeated phrase at the end of the stanzas becomes 'We pushed through for home.'

Like this one, many journeys in the poetry are homecomings. One poem even has the title 'Homecoming', and Armitage's trans-

lation of *Sir Gawain and the Green Knight* and his dramatisation of
the *Odyssey* are both works of homecoming, as is 'True North', where
the speaker is 'hitching home for the first time'. Home remains the
same, but he has changed. The same emotion present at the end of
'An Expedition' appears more prominently in 'The Wood for the
Trees'. In the depths of a rainforest, at 'the furthest point away',
comes the thought of home, 'the long journey backwards'. It pro-
duces 'a sense of calm, and a quietness almost internally near'. In its
way, this anticipates a moment such as the one described near the
end of 'Sir Gawain', when after his travels 'safe and sound he sets
foot in court'.

Conversely, journeys can also be departures from home, such as
the one in 'Mother, any distance . . .'. The speaker climbs to a 'hatch',
the word itself suggesting the beginning of life's journey, and he
finally leaves his mother, 'to fall or fly'. In 'Kid', Robin also moves
away from Batman, as a son might from a father, safe in the knowl-
edge of being 'taller, harder, stronger, older'.

There are also journeys of the imagination. 'A Nutshell', a poem
about wanting a child, jumps from imagining the journey of a ship
being 'put into port' in a bottle to journeys involved in bottling
imaginary fruits, themselves growing in bottles. A comic take on
making a journey to the heart of something is described in 'Man
with a Golf Ball Heart', where the heart is dug out of the body, and
then the investigators go 'further in' to 'that heart'.

On a larger scale, man's evolution is dealt with as a journey in
'Incredible' (based on the science fiction film *The Incredible Shrink-
ing Man*) defeating dangers (sometimes comically, of course) along
the way, such as 'the sparrow in its single-seater plane'. It's 'thought'
that continues to propel him forward, as many of Armitage's jour-
ney poems are really journeys of the imagination, coming home to
a quiet essence, sometimes of 'we', but here 'I'.

Lifetimes went past. With the critical mass
of hardly more than the thought of a thought
I kept on, headlong, to vanishing point.
I looked for an end, for some dimension
to hold hard and resist. But I still exist.

See also (AQA):
'Crossing the Loch' (Kathleen Jamie)
'London' (William Blake)
Extract from 'The Prelude' (William Wordsworth)
'Below the Green Corrie' (Norman MacCaig)
'The Yellow Palm' (Robert Minhinnick)
'At the Border, 1979' (Choman Hardi)
'Belfast Confetti' (Ciaran Carson)
'Come On, Come Back' (Stevie Smith)

Place

'and gives to airy nothing/A local habitation and a name'
  (*A Midsummer Night's Dream*)

A strong sense of place is felt in most of Armitage's poems, whether
as foreground or background. In 'On Miles Platting Station' the
deprived Northern landscape, with its 'near-derelict buildings' and
the 'broken cable', is in the foreground , with the suggestion of a
crime hidden 'behind the windbreak'. 'The shonky side of town' is
the backdrop, but a necessary setting, for the picture of the Clown
Punk. Occasionally the moors, lakes and streams of the poet's own
habitat appear, as in 'Heron', which is 'a fleck on the line of the lake',
beyond which 'the hills are water-marked'. In 'It Ain't What You Do
It's What It Does To You' the speaker relates how he

skimmed flat stones across Black Moss on a day
so still I could hear each set of ripples
as they crossed.

The mention of 'Black Moss' rather than 'the lake', say, is characteristic, and part of a method of fixing the reader's imagination in a particular place, whether imagined or real. 'On Miles Platting Station' is not the only poem to reel off a list of place names, and 'Snow Joke' begins 'Heard the one about the guy from Heaton Mersey?' In 'Missed It by That Much' the couple are placed exactly

> pointing out the landmarks down beneath us,
> me stood, you leant against the trig-point.

While the 'trig-point' may also suggest the pair finding their exact bearings in their relationship at that time, it is also an exact, easily imagined place. The same is true of the positions of the mother and the son in 'Mother any distance'. The mother is 'at the zero end' of the tape measure, but the son is

> Leaving
> up the stairs, the line still feeding out, unreeling
> years between us.

Armitage is also drawn to exotic landscapes, as in 'The Strand' and 'The Wood for the Trees'. The location of the latter is 'the rainforest' and 'a grass hut', populated with exotic flora and fauna, as suggested by the cayman and the 'banana-leaf hat', though the 'quietness' and 'calmness' of home are still closest to his heart.

Often the reader is placed suddenly into a landscape, either real or fictional, and made to imagine it through objects, as in the first stanza of 'Potassium'.

> Finally, under the tree
> with the heart-shaped leaves,
> avoiding the clutches
> of orange insect eggs

Although the 'heart-shaped leaves' and the 'eggs' suggest the beginnings of the new relationship in the rest of the poem, they are also exact descriptions: we can picture where we are.

In 'The Back Man', which begins with a journey through an exotic location, Armitage uses a physical place to explore an inner landscape. The place and the journey have the characteristics of a typical dream or nightmare, walking 'a well-trodden path'. The speaker, the back man in the line, 'saw in my mind's eye' a creature attack him from behind, and after being 'shouldered home in the fibreglass tomb/of a yellow canoe', he 'sat up', 'unharmed' and 'untouched'. The speaker reflects that 'Years on nothing has changed'; he's still the man to be 'hauled down, ripped apart' by a 'sharp backward glance' – not in heroic, exotic situations but in the 'day-to-day'. Danger can appear, or be imagined, on 'Blackstone Edge' or in the 'hotel lobby' or on the escarpment, bringing to mind the paranoia present in other poems. Even in the prosaic location of the barber's chair 'in a sleepy trance', the poet imagines 'some scissor-hand, some needle-finger'.

Place becomes a metaphor for identity in 'Surtsey'. The first part, 'Genesis', charts the development of the island after its creation in 1963 through the advent of 'a microbe' and 'the empires of lichen' to the arrival of man and the arrival of 'the first god' in the shape of a grounded net-float. The second part, 'Where Are They Now?' examines how the island is seen now in very human terms: how has this object, amazing at birth, developed? Armitage was also born in 1963, and the reference in the first two lines to the island as a 'Gifted, precocious sprog', a 'boy-god' brings to mind the Robin of 'Kid', who is now 'the real boy wonder'. Now, 'forty years after our birth', he seems to question whether he, like the island, has 'grown old with grace', or has become one of the 'Lost Child Stars'.

See also (AQA):
'Ozymandias' (Percy Bysshe Shelley)

All the poems in 'Place'
'Mametz Wood' (Owen Sheers)
'At the Border 1979' (Choman Hardi)

Time

'the starting up and slowing down of things' (*This Time Last Year*)

'Look, Stranger!', which is about W. H. Auden and takes its title
from his poem of the same name, deals (as does 'Surtsey') with the
formation of an island, a process which takes time in itself as it
evolves: 'sandbar, reef, atoll'. The sea is a metaphor for time here,
'the sea of the century', into which a stone is skimmed to form an
island. If the island represents the writer ('you went well') and his
growth, this is (unlike in 'Surtsey') fairly well disguised. In 'Novem-
ber', however, time of day is clearly linked to the span of human life:

> Inside, we feel the terror of dusk begin

as the two young men consider the imminent death of the old wom-
an, also suggested in the title. 'Evening', a much more complex poem,
works on the same idea. At 'twelve, thirteen at most' there is 'still time'.
In the second of the four stanzas the tense is future ('one day you'll
learn'), then present ('You fork left'). The beginning of the third stanza
implies that the sun, still present, will set, and then makes this explicit:

> The peak still lit by sun. But
> evening. Evening overtakes you up the slope.
> Dusk walks its fingers up the knuckles of your spine.

This threatening image makes the parallel between time of day and
time of life frighteningly exact. By the last stanza, the child that set
out has a child of its own, a wife, and a sense of incomprehension,
failure and loss worthy of Philip Larkin:

> You're sorry. You thought
> it was early. How did it get so late?

'Evening', though essentially a universal poem, takes care to root the action in a particular place, by naming 'Wool Clough' and 'Royd Edge'. 'The Stone Beach' has an even more concrete sense of place, but here the human family on the beach are placed squarely in the context of time. The 'billion stones and pebbles' still seem new, like 'new potatoes' or 'eggs', but are 'more infinitely formed' than anything human, suggesting already the insignificance of man in the infinity of time. Their 'present tense' only offers a backdating of thirty years, a drop in the ocean of time. They are surrounded by reminders of the effects of time, such as the 'jawbone, bleached/and blasted', while time, in the form of the ocean, proceeds in its even-handed way,

> giving with this, getting back
> with the next.

The reader is reminded of the scope of the canvas of the poem as the disturbed terns make 'one full circle of the world' before the ending insists again on the transient minuteness of man. Reminding us of the skipped stone in 'Surtsey', Jonathan, limited in age and ability ('three, autistic'), has only 'one minute more' in the vast 'flight and fall' of time to cast his stone into the sea of time. His 'last wish' sinks into 'the next wave'.

See also (AQA):
'Ozymandias' (Percy Bysshe Shelley)
'The Blackbird of Glanmore' (Seamus Heaney)
'Cold Knap Lake' (Gillian Clarke)
'The Wild Swans at Coole' (W. B. Yeats)

Language, Structure and Form

This section looks at some of the ways that Simon Armitage uses language, structure and form to contribute to meaning in his poetry.

Language

In many of his poems Armitage creates voice and immediacy by using the vocabulary and conventions of everyday speech, often deliberately modern, or Northern, or both.

The language of the North

Northern street language is often in evidence, as in:

> He had a hair up his arse
> at the best of times ('All Beer and Skittles')
>
> you're scuppered before you've even started ('Ten Pence Story')
>
> That Monday had been a proper scorcher ('B and B')
>
> He was spark out ('Defrosting a Chicken')
>
> And every week he tipped up half his wage ('Poem')

There are dialect grammatical usages as well as dialect vocabulary:

> That's him sat down, not like those other clowns ('Goalkeeper with a Cigarette')

In the same poem, Northern vowel sounds dominate, as in

> with hands as stunted as a bunch of thumbs

In Armitage's poetry, first-person poems can be his own voice or the creation of another character. Occasionally dialect is rendered phonetically, to capture an exact voice, as in 'On an Owd Piktcha'.

The brew of dialect sound and contemporary slang and reference is powerfully in evidence in the five poems entitled 'Sympathy', which examine victims.

> Anyways, on t'morning after t'party
> I trogs downstairs, still bolloxed, and gives t'pantry
> t'Hans Blix, lookin' for brain-numbin' drugs.

The narrative voice in 'Sir Gawain' seems to have Northern origins, too. The green knight's axe is described as 'a cruel piece of kit, I kid you not', and Gawain himself as 'a namby-pamby knight' by his green challenger.

The common touch

Several poems use or refer to common phrases in the titles, such as 'And You Know What Thought Did', 'All Beer and Skittles', and 'It Ain't What You Do It's What It Does To You'. Occasionally these kick-start the poem by using the first line to complete the sentence. 'Never Mind the Quality' is followed by 'feel the width', and 'Before You Cut Loose' by 'put dogs on the list'.

Common phrases are used to establish voice and attitude. 'It's not much to crow about' and 'me ready to stir it' are examples of this in 'True North', as is

> How very fly of him,
> the father of the skies ('Cover Version')

In 'Surtsey', modern words and idiom locate the situation in the second part of the poem: when the speaker is 'winched down under the rotor-blade', he wonders if he will find 'bum-fluffed brain-boxed kids in National Health specs'.

Some poems centre on language itself, as do 'All Beer and Skittles' and 'The Stuff', both of which tell their stories through strings

of common expressions. 'Ivory' is about the language of speech, and
begins

> No more malarkey,
> no baloney

'The Metaphor Now Standing at Platform 8' plays with the idea of
metaphor, wrapped up in the language and imagery of trains: 'a boy/
could do worse than be a spotter of metaphors'. The last three lines,
in the voice of the conductor (and therefore of the poet who writes
the metaphor) tracks through three speech phrases and into a last
sentence which glances at film fiction speech:

> This is a metaphor I'm running here
> not a jamboree, and as soon as we get that straight
> we're rolling. Till then, no one goes nowherè.

'B and B' begins 'It's easier than falling off a log', and 'Bempton' with
the lines:

> Things have come
> to this pretty pass:

The poem is a rural one, about a 'pretty pass' literally, and ends
'That old chestnut.' Armitage uses the phrases here playfully, to grab
the reader's attention through the language twist, but also as a direct,
colloquial way of catapulting us into the situation. Similarly, 'Ten
Pence Story' begins 'Out of the melting pot, into the mint', this time
intriguing the reader by changing a known expression to suit the
story of the coin. 'Going West' uses the same technique to describe
an argument:

> we point and counterpoint,
> tread a thin line,
> split hairs so finely
> that we lose the thread.

In 'D Notice', which is a term describing government prohibition of a news story, Armitage plays with five different expressions in three lines in the course of making his point about being silenced:

> To tie
> the tongue instead of wagging it,
> clamp the jaw, put
> a sock not a foot in it

In 'Homecoming' there is a similar quick slide through expressions, this time showing how a mother jumps to conclusions:

> puts
> two and two together, makes a proper fist of it
> and points the finger.

'Seeing Stars' takes the 'casual metaphor' for what happens after receiving 'a blow on the head', identifies it as such, and then explores it. The chemist who is the narrator of the poem is attacked after he asks the couple demanding heroin to 'think of the baby' because the woman has requested a pregnancy-testing kit. He sees

> 'Whole galaxies of
> stars, and planets orbiting around them, each one capable of
> sustaining life as we know it. I waved from the porthole of
> my interstellar rocket as I hurtled past, and from inside
> their watery cocoons millions of helpless half-formed
> creatures with doughy faces and pink translucent fingers
> waved back.'

'Seeing stars', 'capable of sustaining life as we know it' combine to create the image of the man in the rocket, and the eerie picture of the waving foetuses.

Playing with Language

As in several of the examples above, Armitage constantly plays with the sounds and meanings of words to shift the reader's mind from one idea to another, linking them to make new meanings. On the simplest level, this can be with a single word, such as 'in my butter-fingered way' in 'I am very bothered when I think'. 'Butterfingered' here makes the reader think of clumsiness, but also of butter placed on the fingers to soothe a burn. Sound and meaning is used across two lines in 'In Our Tenth Year':

> your inventory of names and dates and times,
> my infantries of tall, dark, handsome lies.

'Infantries' picks up and changes the word 'inventory', which is in the same position in the previous line, linking the idea of a number of soldiers, male and inferior, and also suggesting 'infant', as one or both of the partners might see the male figure.

The speed of these verbal shifts can sometimes signal speed of action. The row between the mother and daughter in 'Homecoming' is captured quickly:

> You seeing red. Blue murder. Bed.

This technique looks very easy, but is carefully formed. 'Seeing red' and 'blue murder' are common enough expressions, but here the colour shifts rapidly from red to blue, 'red' and 'murder' chime in meaning and letters, and 'blue and 'bed' form an alliteration. The three-letter words 'red' and bed' rhyme within the line, and the sentences move from three words to two to one, suggesting a short, sharp and abruptly ended exchange.

The speed of a story unfolding is suggested in the same way throughout 'C.V.', beginning with the opening stanza:

> Started, textiles, night shift,
> no wheels, bussed it,
> bus missed, thumbed it,
> in my office sunbeam, fluffed it.

Word sounds and meanings work in 'The Stuff'.

> Someone bubbled us. C.I.D. sussed us
> and found some on us. It was cut and dried

Working within the language of the drug trade and street crime, the lines work though the chiming of 'bubbled' and 'sussed', the rhythm of the line falling on the two vowels, which then echo for the third time in 'us' before the full stop. This in itself makes the discovery seem 'cut and dried', an expression which also carries an association with the powdered drug. The relentless forward motion of 'A Week and a Fortnight' is driven with the working together of alliteration, rhythm and rhyme:

> Fed with the fur not the flesh of a peach
> but bruised in the garden, tripped in the street,
> bunged with a bottle of petrol and bleach.

Metaphor

Armitage often uses strings of metaphors, either extending a metaphor over several lines or shades of meaning (which is termed a conceit), or using several metaphors to evoke the same thing. In 'Mother, any distance greater than a single span' the measuring tape used to measure 'windows, pelmets, doors' becomes a measure of the difference in their relationship as the son grows older: 'unreeling/ years between us'. 'Anchor. Kite' transforms the tape into a chain or rope, at once securing the son and holding him back, and 'feeding out' in the previous line now makes the reader sense the umbilical cord, which is then stretched 'to breaking point, where something has to give', as the son cuts himself free from the mother, literally and metaphorically. The end of the poem sees the metaphor stretched again, and then changed:

> Two floors below your fingertips still pinch
> the last one-hundredth of an inch . . . I reach
> towards a hatch that opens on an endless sky
> to fall or fly.

The 'spool of tape' has run from line 5 to this moment, with the mother clinging on to the connection, broken by the ellipsis (. . .). The 'hatch' is literal, but the reader, alive to metaphor in this poem, is likely to associate 'hatch' with a new birth, and independence – but a dangerous independence – from the mother. The egg metaphor suggests that the chick will either 'fall or fly'.

In 'I've made out a will, I'm leaving myself' Armitage compares the workings and elements of the body to the innards of a grandfather clock across four lines of the poem, then concludes it with:

> but not the pendulum, the ticker;
> leave that where it stops or hangs.

'The ticker' beautifully combines the clock image with the heart itself, which brings death firmly into the last line. Earlier in the poem Armitage offers three different metaphors for the skeleton: 'The chassis or cage or cathedral of bone.' Here the poet seems to hold up the object to the light for the reader, showing it in three different ways, with different connotations. In 'Ankylosing spondylitis' Armitage again describes the body as 'clockwork', with a string of mechanical metaphors, but fears that his 'skeleton will set like biscuit overnight,/like glass, like ice' – again offering three metaphors, this time for fragility.

In 'Homecoming', as in 'Mother, any distance', an object, this time a 'canary-yellow cotton jacket' is transformed into an extended metaphor. The 'pleats', 'sleeves', 'buttons' and 'buckle' of the jacket become the ribs, arms, and fingers of the speaker of the poem, and finally the putting on again of the jacket becomes a metaphor for trust, and the closeness of love:

> Step backwards into it
> and try the same canary-yellow cotton jacket, there,
> like this, for size again. It still fits.

Language, through the form of the central metaphor, has defined the poem and tied it up finally. Similarly, a simile at the beginning of one of the 'Book of Matches' poems defines the life of the speaker and starts the journey of the poem:

> People never push me into doing things
> I don't want to do. So I go like a railway guard

The poem works its way through a number of variations of life as a railway journey, as seen through the eyes of this personality, reaching a haunting conclusion about the passing of life:

> I shall sit, to see from here the signals
> changing, to say nothing
> of the parallel lines converging, and fading.

In 'An Accommodation', the net curtain draped across the middle of the room to separate the estranged couple becomes a metaphor for the disintegration of their relationship:

> Over the years the moths moved in, got a taste for
> the net, so it came to resemble a giant web, like a
> thing made of actual holes strung together by fine,
> nervous threads. But there it remained, and remains
> to this day, this tattered shroud, this ravaged lace
> suspended between our lives, keeping us
> inseparable and betrothed.

The relationship, like the net, is 'ravaged', 'tattered', and consists more in holes than substance, but also keeps them 'inseparable', as though they are tied to it. The couple seem like an imagined Mr and Mrs Havisham, simultaneously bound to each other, separated and damaged.

'Not the Furniture Game' uses strings of metaphor in a completely different way. Each one of the first 44 lines of the poem is a metaphor, beginning 'His hair was a crow fished out of a blocked chimney'. The long string of metaphors builds up a picture of the man's strength and size, as in 'his nostrils were both barrels of a shotgun, loaded' and 'his grin was the Great Wall of China'. The two metaphors at the end of the poem, as they are delivered over two lines each, destroy both the pattern, and the sense of strength: she is 'a chair, tipped over backwards', and his face now 'a hole' of weakness, the exact opposite of what has gone before.

Personification is used very strikingly in 'Harmonium' and 'To Poverty'. 'Harmonium' is concerned with the age of the father figure, and the harmonium's case has 'yellowed the fingernails of its keys', an idea picked up later in the poem with the mention of the father's 'smoker's fingers and dottled thumbs'. 'To Poverty' personifies poverty as a familiar acquaintance of the speaker: they are 'joined at the pocket'.

Structure

Openings

A number of Armitage's poems begin in the middle of an event or conversation, inviting the reader to catch up quickly, or suggesting that they are overhearing the speaker. 'Poem by the Boy Outside the Fire Station' begins 'Anyway, I'm mad', and 'Gooseberry Season 'Which reminds me.' 'An Accommodation' begins with the omission of a name, marked by a dash:

– and I both agreed that something had to change.

First lines of some poems carry on directly from the title. 'Before You Cut Loose' continues

> put dogs on the list

The continuation is marked by the position of the line on the page, and the lower-case first letter.

Lists

Several poems are shaped around lists, of things or events. 'About His Person' lists items in pockets, and ends simply 'That was everything'. 'Poem' lists things that the subject of the poem did, and summarises the list in the last line:

> sometimes he did this, sometimes he did that.

'Not the Furniture Game' works through a long list of metaphors describing one person, then switches to one metaphor describing the other person in the relationship, and ends on a final metaphor which is quite opposite in tone from the rest.

Journeys

Many of Armitage's poems are structured around journeys. The longer narrative poems, *Sir Gawain and the Green Knight* and the *Odyssey* clearly do this in forming a narrative, but the shorter poems often string events or places together quickly and come to a point of stasis, which may be a return home, or the thought of home. 'An Expedition', for instance, which is an imaginary and comic trip around decorating, ends

> we pushed through for home.

'Home' here both ends the journey and transforms it into a more serious sense, of the completion of a concept, not just a roll of wallpaper. In 'The Wood for the Trees' the speaker is in an exotic location, with most of the poem built around injunctions to 'Trust in' various sayings or reassurances; but when thoughts of 'the long journey backwards' occur, a moment of stasis and change arrives in the last couplet, the full rhyme accentuating the harmony of the moment:

> and a quietness almost internally near,
> Then distant thoughts were suddenly blindingly clear.

'Zoom!', which opens 'It begins as a house' comes to a clear stop with 'But they will not have it.' The list of jobs in 'C.V.', tumbling over each other quickly in truncated phrases, ends with:

> or out to grass, find door to lay me at.

The journey in 'The Tyre' starts a little way into the poem, at 'we drove it', and although the journey does have a completion, at the same time the conclusion is unknown:

> and at that moment gone beyond itself
> towards some other sphere, and disappeared.

Occasionally poems are framed by repetitions of openings in the endings, such as 'Lest We Forget', which is structured around lists of forgotten or endangered places and incidentals associated with Huddersfield. The first two verses of the litany are repeated as the last two, to drive home the idea perhaps, while in repeating the names giving them a continuing existence. 'Fire' begins

> We could not see it from the cemetery

and ends

> from the cemetery we could not see it.

Sometimes the ending of a poem flows from a point of balance in the middle, like a fulcrum. The words 'Anchor. Kite', for instance, in the poem 'Mother, any distance greater than a single span' occur in the centre of the poem, followed by a stanza break. This allows the reader to pause before the second half of the poem. The first half is inhabited by 'us', but the second by 'I', the son who is climbing away from his mother, literally and metaphorically. 'Anchor. Kite' are balanced by 'to fall or fly' as the last line, on its own, the two balanced opposites reflecting the words in the centre of the poem and placed in the same order, the kite hoping to fly. Similarly, in 'Gooseberry Season' the first half of the poem details the stranger's visit, and the second half what happens to him. In the centre comes the line:

> Where does the hand become the wrist?

as the speaker muses on the moment when thought becomes action, here precipitating a murder.

Endings

Summing up

In the same way that some poems begin as lines from traditional jokes ('Heard the one about the man from Heaton Mersey?' or 'I say I say I say'), some end with punchlines, such as

> If you only pay peanuts, you're working with monkeys. ('Eighties, Nineties')

Often a series of statements running through a poem will reach a concluding thought at the end of the poem, which might summarise the thinking or move it to a different level. In 'I am able to keep my mind', for instance, the descriptions of skimming stones leads to the final moment of

> Drop down
> Into a wider world.

In 'The Stuff' the drug addict's story recaps the events of the poem by offering a repeated word from each of its stages, as a sort of précis, before ending with a typical Armitage flourish:

> I said grapevine, barge pole, whirlpool, chloride,
> concrete, bandage, station, story. Honest.

The last word not only echoes speech, but makes the reader reflect on what has gone before: honest or not? Similar endings can define the characters presented in the poems. In 'The Ornithologists', the tidy, cataloguing cast of mind suggested in the preceding thoughts is caught exactly in the last two lines:

> It's how to live. Minds should be like houses:
> clean, open and in order like ours is.

In the same way, 'hard freight' sums up the no-nonsense character presented in 'People talk nonsense and I put them straight'.

Some poems end with a moment or an image which symbolises what has gone before. In 'Working with the Mussel Farmers', for instance, the amorous fishing couple are suggested in the quaintly erotic conclusion:

> I part and sample their famous shellfish,
> strange in flavour
> perfect in appearance.

In 'Map Reference' the last line – 'That it stood where it stood, so absolutely, for you' – sums up the conceit that runs through the poem of the female figure as a nondescript landmark. Similarly, but with a very different effect on the reader, the last line of 'Penelope':

> I mark the best bloom, take it at the neck

refers to the flower which has become a symbol of Penelope 'in a rich, deep bed' . The gardener, who has seemed to be simply watching over Penelope until her husband's return, now seems like a voyeur, and a dangerous one, through the power of the final image. A different relationship is suggested through a metaphor in the final line of 'Ice'. The speaker, who feels 'I am to blame', stands outside the house watching the bathwater run from the pipe and noting that

> Already its edges
> are beginning to harden
> – like the relationship itself, perhaps.

The final line of 'Those bastards in their mansions' is a summing-up, in a sense: it captures the speaker's situation and attitude in a one-line sentence, separated from the rest of the poem, in the same way as the speaker is a solitary, separated figure:

> Me, I stick to the shadows, carry a gun.

Balancing

The last lines sometimes offer a moment of balance between one thing and another, perhaps in a balanced line such as 'to fall or fly' at the end of 'Mother, any distance', or 'sometimes he did this, sometimes he did that' at the end of 'Poem'. At the end of 'In Our Tenth Year' the ups and downs of a relationship are suggested through the poem by 'disagreements' and 'lies' on the one hand, and 'twinned but doubled now with love' on the other. The giving of a harebell, itself an object suggesting fragility, provides an ending where the life and death of the relationship can be contained in one image, and in language which employs four balancing words and phrases:

> Let's give it now
> in air, with light, the chance to fade, to fold.
> Here, take it from my hand. Now, let it go.

'But he don't. So he do' is a much simpler example of this (from
'There are those who manage their private affairs').

A balanced final line, as a way of musically concluding a poem, is
a common feature. 'Don't leave me be. Don't let me sleep' captures
the desperation of the speaker in 'ankylosing spondylitis' and 'wait-
ing for t'exit wound, waiting for t'blood to pump' is the disturbing
last line of one of the 'Sympathy' poems, and

> if that divides
> by this, or this by that, or that by this

forms the incantatory finish to 'Self-Portrait'. Similarly, 'The
Hard', which details the steps to death of a stranger caught out by
the tide on an unfamiliar coastline, ends in a line of three threaten-
ing steps:

> it tells us how taken you are,
> how carried away by now, how deep and how far.

Another poem that specifically finishes with a moment of weighing
is 'A Hip Flask':

> tailored, weighed
> and measured, worked both ways, this present made
> to hide the heart and hold the heart in place.

As in several other poems, this final, serious line to end an otherwise
jokey poem leads to the heart: 'the heart, the ticker'.

'A Week and a Fortnight' ends in counting and balancing. The
first six of the seven three-line stanzas detail one 'good' occurrence
and two 'bad', then the seventh reverses this with one 'bad' followed
by two 'good', as in

> Left for an hour with booze and a razor
> but carted by ambulance clear of the woods
> saved at the last by drugs and a laser.

The last verse reveals the scheme and the meaning of the lines to the reader in three balanced lines, each longer than the last:

> Days for the dirty, life for the lost,
> the acts of mercy and the stations of the cross
> the seven acts of mercy and the fourteen stations of the cross.

'You're Beautiful' balances statements about 'You' being beautiful and 'I' being ugly throughout, and in this poem there is a refrain in italics, cleverly weaving together the pronouns 'he', his', her', and hers', and this forms the ending of the poem. The capital letters for each line are unusual for Armitage, and reflect the almost formal feel of the refrain, like a chorus or a chant.

> *Ugly like he is,*
> *Beautiful like hers*
> *Beautiful like Venus*
> *Ugly like his,*
> *Beautiful like she is,*
> *Ugly like hers.*

Moments that transcend, or challenge

Sometimes Armitage's poems end with moments that challenge the reader, or take the mind suddenly in a new, unexpected direction. 'Well, here I am' ('The Middle Distance') is a challenge, as is 'try looking a dog like that in the eye' ('Before You Cut Loose'). In 'The Short Way Home'

> could you
> settle for as much? Could you live with it?

is a very direct challenge, and there is a strong sense of threat to the other character in 'The Two of Us' in the final line, broken away from the rest of the poem to increase the sense of a direct personal attack:

because the worm won't know your make of bone from mine.

The structure of a day and a life that runs alarmingly quickly through 'Evening' works chillingly to the simple word 'late', with everything that it implies:

> You thought
> it was early. How did it get so late?

A shift into a different picture is apparent at the end of 'A Meteorite', when

> this rock becomes a gem,
> a gift; your fingers open slowly, like
> a flower, from a fist. As if. As if.

'The Experience' is a comic piece about grave-robbing featuring a character who happens to be called Richard Dawkins, but ends with strange and rather troubling moments – first the discovery of a goose in a coffin, then the appearance of a fox,

> A silent, man-size fox in a dark frockcoat and long black
> gloves, standing up on its hind legs, watching.

Even more troubling is the vision of the bear at the end of 'Beyond Huddersfield'. The bear seen hunting through mounds of trash is an unpleasant picture, but the imaginary leap in the last line takes this to a nastier level entirely, as the bear is seen with,

> the gleaming needle digging for the sunken vein.

a move from environmental issues to anthropological.

Form

Different shapes/forms

From the beginning of his career as a published poet, Armitage experimented with form. In his first collection, *Zoom!* (1989), poems

appeared in stanzas of 2-, 3-, 4- or 5-line lengths, and often ended
with a 2-line stanza in rhyme or half-rhyme, or a single line. These
forms have remained staples, but successive collections marked fur-
ther experimentation, such as a series of indented lines in the middle
of a stanza. In *Kid* (1992), 'Eighteen Plays on Golfing as a Watch-
word' has a collection of stanzas of different lengths for each hole.

In *Book of Matches* (1993) a wider range of forms appear. The title
sequence is a series of poems that play with sonnet form (see below).
'The Lost Letter of the Late Jud Fry' has stanzas of five lines in
length, that begin and end in a single word:

> Yours –
> That's him for sure.
> The sun will have its day,
> its weeks, months,
> years.

These jagged, pointed short lines catch the studied, smouldering
nature of the character. More poems appear in this collection with
irregular stanzas, the length of each being matched to the length of
the thought or event being described. The collection ends with a
sequence entitled 'Reading the Banns' – twelve short poems, all in
two-line stanzas, describing a couple who are getting married.

In *CloudCuckooLand* (1997) the poem 'Good Ship Melancholia' has
stanzas of 5, 4, 3 and 2 lines sequentially, leading to a moment which
is quite different to what has gone before – a moment of change. Most
of the collection is taken up with a long sequence, 'The Whole of the
Sky', which uses the shapes of different constellations as points of
reference that attempt to structure human and earthly activities.

Further radical experimentation appears in *The Universal Home
Doctor* (2002), particularly in 'The Flags of the Nations' and 'Assault
on the Senses'. In the former, a left-hand column on the page has a
list of types of coloured bag used for the disposal of hospital waste

material, and the right-hand column offers definitions of the words. In 'Assault on the Senses' definitions are given of entries in an imaginary art exhibition. Both of these poems look like prose pieces on the page, and in doing so start to evade traditional notions of form. In this way they anticipate *Seeing Stars* (2010), which consists of prose-like pieces which are also poems: the form has become difficult to define.

This sense of reaching out to different forms of expression is also the background, perhaps, to Armitage's work in translating *Sir Gawain and the Green Knight* and dramatising *Homer's Odyssey* into modern language. The collection *Tyrannosaurus Rex and the Corduroy Kid* (2006) features an even wider range of form. It begins with a poem in the form of a numbered list, 'Hand-Washing Technique – Government Guidelines'. Like 'The Flags of the Nations', this is a 'found' poem, reproduced verbatim from an original sign or poster. 'You're Beautiful' experiments with a refrain, repeated at the end. 'Sympathy' is a sequence of five poems in which an event is described in the first five lines and followed by a response in dialect, printed in italics, after an asterisk in the text. The responses are arranged in two stanzas of ten lines, followed by a single last line rounding off the thought. 'Surtsey' is a poem in two parts, while 'Bayeux Tapestry' has lines arranged in two columns, justified to left and right with a gap in the centre, so that the lines appear stretched, like the tapestry in the title. 'Pheasants' is divided into sections mirroring the birds: 'Hen', 'Cock', 'Brace' and 'Flock'. In 'Learning by Rote' each line is written backwards (apart from a repetition of 'Simon Armitage, Simon Armitage'), so that the words become almost impossible to read. Perhaps learning by rote makes no sense. The poem can be read by holding a mirror to the margin; this reveals the speaker's resentment about copying words out backwards as a punishment for being left-handed.

A further experiment with form is evident in *The Not Dead* (2008), which presented poems written for a television documentary about soldiers who are haunted in some way by what happened to them in conflict. The lines are all centred, giving a rather regimented appearance.

Sonnets

A sonnet is a poem of fourteen lines, usually written in iambic pentameter, with a clear rhyme scheme. Like many poets, Armitage is attracted to the discipline of the sonnet as a form of expression – and to challenging that discipline. Typically, he plays continually with the form for effect. This is clearly in evidence in the title sequence of poems in *Book of Matches*. Each of these poems has an asterisk instead of a title, to represent the flare of a match struck by the speaker, as he or she tells the story of their lives. The first poem sets out the method, and also the intention to push the envelope of the conventional form. The poem is split into four stanzas. Others can have three or four, and the last in the sequence has five. There is only one rhyme in the poem, in lines 9 and 11. The lines are of unequal length, and after line 14 a single word is added as line 15, 'madness', as though it is a physical expression of detachment or difference.

Most of the poems in the sequence have 14 lines, though 'Mother, any distance greater than a single span' also spreads into line 15, this time with three words:

> I reach
> towards a hatch that opens on an endless sky
> to fall or fly.

The words are attached by the rhyme, but seem to 'fall or fly' off the poem, as the son takes off in one direction or another.

Most of the poems in the sequence have irregular line lengths, including lines of one word, such as 'Pull!' in 'I am able to keep my mind steadily', capturing the pulling back of the arm and the pause before throwing and skimming a stone. Line 4 of 'I'm dreaming of that work' consists of 'me' – a single word, to match the situation of the speaker being alone in the world. The final word of 'The story changes every time' is 'suicide', in a last line on its own.

Rhyme and half-rhyme are used sparingly in these poems, but always to match a mood or tone, or to make a point. 'People talk nonsense and I put them straight', for instance, ends:

> People talk nonsense
> so I put them straight, and I carry no passengers, just
> hard freight.

'Freight' not only rhymes with 'straight' in the previous line but also with 'straight' in the first, in the very ordered world of the speaker here. Similarly, 'I'm dreaming of that work' finishes

> I lock and latch
> and bar and bolt the windows and the hatch.

The regular rhyme and the steady, insistent rhythm here capture the speaker's need for the safety, perhaps, of being locked down.

Occasionally Armitage moves much closer to a traditional form, as if to show that he can do it when he wants to, as in 'My father thought it bloody queer', with its lines of 5 or 6 beats and sets of rhyme and half-rhyme, though 'skin' and 'friend' are little more than an echo.

Several times the poems end with a single line split from the rest of the poem, to create a moment of drama. 'Ankylosing spondylitis', for instance, ends:

> the shape I take becomes the shape I keep.
> Don't leave me be. Don't let me sleep.

The full stops here, the isolation of the line, and the keep/sleep rhyme work together to make the desperate statements more stark and affecting.

Rants and Litanies

Several poems read like rants by characters, creating the mood and tone of the speakers. In 'Kid', for instance, Robin's angry tone, caught by 'Batman, big shot' in the opening, is maintained throughout by the rhyming or chiming final words on each line, which all conclude with 'er', as in 'wander' and 'yonder'. These 'feminine endings' keep the reader tumbling through the 24 lines of the poem to the exultant portrayal of Batman at the end of the poem

> punching the palm of your hand all winter,
> you baby, now I'm the real boy wonder.

'Killing Time #2' also builds up a head of steam as the clipped words and phrases capture the pace of modern life.

> Don't dilly dally or the trail goes cold, sir,
> don't hold back till you're mouldy old dough, sir,
>   sprint for the line,
>   turn on a dime;
> sit tight, hang fire, I'm putting you on hold, sir,
>   too late, snail pace, already sold, sir,
> blame it on the kids but it's you getting old, sir.

These lines, with their easy use of phrases drawn from the idioms of contemporary speech, their relentless use of rhymes and echoes, and the short lines to create pace could only be Armitage. 'Song of the West Men', describing the wearying ordeal of a fisherman who managed to survive falling into the sea and an epic journey to land, captures the event by using repetition throughout, together with the same sort of techniques of sound, rhythm and line length as 'Killing Time':

> He met with the land
> where the cliffs of the cliffs

> were steeper than sheer
> where the sheep had to graze
> by the teeth of their teeth.

'Lest We Forget' is a litany of names, heaped on each other to emphasise the scope of what has been lost, or might be:

> Engels, Duke, the Domesday Book,
> Aspin, Beaumont, Copper, Wood,
> mungo, shoddy, scribble, fud . . .

'To His Lost Lover' is a list of things that never happened, in rhyming or half-rhyming couplets, many romantic or comic mishaps. The litany ends with a deep sense of failure, however:

> And left unsaid some things he should have spoken,
> about the heart, where it hurt exactly, and how often.

Biography, with some questions and answers

This section intersperses some biographical details about Simon Armitage with some question and answers from Simon about his life and work.

Simon Armitage was born in Marsden in West Yorkshire in 1963.

Question: Several of your poems mention Marsden directly. Is the village important to you?

Answer: Yes. I think that in a lot of ways it is the epicentre of my poetry. Many actually start from Marsden, such as the house in 'Zoom!', even though I don't actually identify it as such, or are written from the perspective of a bedroom window in the house I grew up in. In some ways the place is a template for all of my writing, a system of thinking – the world seen through the filter of Marsden, if you like. I spent my formative years in the village, staring at the railway line that stretched away to the east or buried into the hill to the west, observing the workings of the roads and shops, like a watch with the back taken off. I could see the borders between Yorkshire and Lancashire, between rural and urban, and between private and public, and positioned myself in the margins in between, which is a good place for a writer to be. Amphibious, I guess, commuting between one medium and another.

Armitage first studied at Colne Valley High School, Linthwaite, Huddersfield.

Question: Not many of your poems seem to deal with school life directly, which is surprising given its influence on most people. Was school life important to you, in retrospect?

Answer: There are some poems based in school experience, such as 'The Shout' and 'The Straight and Narrow'. I found secondary school quite an alienating experience. It was huge, and easy to get lost – easy too, and in fact necessary, to drift away from the mainstream. I don't think there were many opportunities for an individual, in the sense that teaching attention had to be spread more widely. Besides which, it wasn't a good idea to be too prominent, and I learned how to be small, invisible, silent. The result of this ethos was the opening up of subcultures, of having an alternative mindset. It was another way of being on the margins, expressed through things like music choice. I think that I've mythologised a lot of my school experience, perhaps because now I can say what it was like for me, I've gained some control over it – which I didn't have at the time – by writing about it.

Question: Although there aren't many poems about school, there are more about your parents. The poems aren't quite what one would expect from a writer who was 'at the margins', though: there doesn't seem to be much sense of rebellion and conflict. Even 'My father thought it bloody queer' is tinged with affection.

Answer: Put simply, it's probably because I was lucky enough to have good parents. While not being liberal in the sense that 'anything went', they were still quite hands off, so I didn't have much to kick against. It's true that there was a bit of unrest when I first returned from college with a certain swagger and plenty to say for myself, which is the period of 'My father thought it bloody queer', but it didn't last long. A number of my poems could be described as 'rites of passage' poems, but they tend to be about smaller ritualistic transitions rather than full-scale revolution.

I've noticed that some of the poems about my father have a rather elegiac quality, where I take the position of looking back, in a sort of pre-commemorative way. It's always hard to praise or to thank someone, and maybe those poems are a way of saying it in advance! My father is very well known in these parts; to most people around here I will always be his son, and that perspective is apparent in some of the poems.

> Armitage has lived all his life so far in West Yorkshire.

Question: You've always lived in the North. Is that important to your poetry?

Answer: I suppose it must be. I think I have a Northern outlook and attitude, which can manifest itself in taking the position of the underdog, for example, and a kind of truculence: independence, perhaps, and a deliberate disconnection from the establishment. So yes, I'm a Northern poet, without feeling required to represent the North in a professional way, like turning up at readings in a flat cap eating a block of lard. I do sometimes mock or play up to Northern stereotypes, such as in 'The Two of Us' and 'The Laughing Stock', and even in 'Those bastards in their mansions'. It's my prerogative, and on occasions I take advantage of it.

Question: In many of your poems your sympathy seems to be with the working class. Some students have seen you as a class warrior. Is that how you see yourself?

Answer: I wouldn't be comfortable with the idea of my work being reduced to a simple political point of view, but I am a product of my background, so there are times when I find myself giving expression to it. But then, putting words on the page is a political act, because in Britain just to open your mouth is an expression of social and geographical circumstances.

Question: Even though you're a dyed-in-the-wool Northerner, you do seem attracted to journeys: your poems are full of them.

Answer: West Yorkshire feels like a sound and secure base, a good place to set off from and come back to. It's a solid foundation. I'd like to go to the Moon – who wouldn't? – but only if I could come back here and tell people what it was like. I believe in communities, but only if the door is open, so that people can come and go as they please.

> Armitage studied Geography at Portsmouth Polytechnic.

Question: Some students might suppose that a poet would have studied English Literature in Higher Education. Would it have made a difference to you if you'd done that?

Answer: Yes, a negative difference. I was very contrary at that age; I would have reacted against Literature if I'd been made to study it formally. While I was studying Geography, I was writing and reading in my own way, and in my own time. It was a private journey and a secret activity.

> Until 1994 he worked as a Probation Officer in Greater Manchester.

Question: What effect did this job have on your view of the world, and on your work?

Answer: I was brought face to face with the nuts and bolts of other people's lives, lives very unlike my own. It seemed another brutal world, like school but far worse, and equally difficult to accept or understand. Poetry was an escape, a personal indulgence. The experiences were often shocking and difficult to make sense of. Maybe the poems were a way of reacting to those experiences on a personal and introspective level rather than through professional guidelines or the cold language of the law.

Question: In 1995 you gave up your job to be a full-time writer. Was this an easy decision for you to make?

Answer: To leave the Probation Service? No, it was difficult and painful. Financially it was obviously a risk, putting aside a professional qualification I'd worked four years for, and a secure job with a salary and pension when I already had obligations and responsibilities. I could have been giving it up for a fantasy. And artistically there were risks attached too: I didn't know how much poetry I had in me, especially if I was no longer in the 'real' world of conventional work. What if I came downstairs on Monday morning having declared myself to be a poet, only to find I had nothing to say?

Question: Given the difficulties, why did you decide to do it?

Answer: Would you rather be a poet or a probation officer? More seriously, I think I'd been following my head for a long time, and decided to follow my heart instead. It's what I wanted to do.

Question: Who were the early influences in your poetry that helped you to find your own voice as a poet?

Answer: More than anything, the poetry of Ted Hughes. One of the interesting things about finding my own poems in GCSE anthologies is that I first discovered his poems at exactly the same age, working for exams in school. I remember reading poems like 'Bayonet Charge' and being struck by these moments of direct experience that seemed to be speaking directly to me. They were like little acts of magic, making the experiences happen by stimulating every sense through the words. That early connection is still with me, I think. I tuned in to it straight away, and knew that I wanted to read more poetry like it, rather than write it at that stage. This passion felt like my secret for a long time, something that I kept on the side, so that I did a Geography degree rather than English, and an MA in Psychology. I suppose I see myself as a home-made poet, in that sense.

Reading Hughes inevitably led me to other poets, often found in second-hand bookshops, so that I was reading what other people had thrown away, but I valued. These were Thom Gunn, then Heaney, then Larkin. I also found American voices in *An Anthology of American Verse*. I particularly liked the poems from the late fifties and sixties, because they sounded like people talking rather than writing in a 'literary' sort of way. They seemed to have a real relationship to voice, to colloquial expression, much more so than most of the British writing of the period; this seemed quite radical to me. Frank O'Hara appealed to me a great deal. He seemed to deal with domestic, everyday experience in a way that allowed the reader to see wider meaning.

Question: I find it interesting that a poet's job is to articulate experience, but often you confess in the poems that you can't find the words to express emotion. Is that a contradiction?

Answer: Sometimes there's a *feeling* you want to express, but for all its sophistications language is too blunt an instrument to describe it.

'That feeling, I mean' might be an example of that, in the poem 'It Ain't What You Do . . .'. Added to which, I always try to avoid sentimentality, which is why the speaker in some of the poems might be willing to tell you so much, then no more.

Question: You seem to like playing with meanings, with the sounds of words, and with form. Do you see the process of writing that way?

Answer: It certainly can feel like solving a puzzle, or doing a cryptic crossword; and the more formal the poem, the more game-playing takes place. Or like a competition between me and the poem, one I've got to win. In that sense, writing poems is not the fluent and spontaneous act I'd once hoped it would become, but it's always engrossing and engaging. The main struggle is to compose the sound and create the shape of a poem, because in the end they are its defining characteristics, the ones by which it will live or die.

> In addition to poetry, Simon writes for radio, television and film, and is the author of four stage plays and two novels

Question: Which of these writing forms do you enjoy most?

Answer: Poetry, no question. That's what I want to do, the thing I feel most love and loyalty towards. It's what I'm proudest of, what I want to be known for. And it's cool to be a poet, right? But you can't work at that pitch all the time, sustaining the level of intensity and concentration that poetry requires, so a more general urge to write or work with language leads in other directions. Prose, for example. Or drama, or song lyrics.

Question: You're very interested in music, too, to the extent of having your own band, The Scaremongers. How does that fit into the writing equation?

Answer: The music is a diversion and a recreation, and even though song-writing and poetry-writing share a few techniques they are, at the end of the day, distinct and unconnected activities. I certainly can't do both at the same time! If I'm writing poetry I need silence, because if there's a song playing I'll start listening to the music of the song, not the music of the poem. I agree with George Mackay Brown, who described poetry as 'the interrogation of silence'.

> Simon Armitage has lectured on creative writing at the University of Leeds, the University of Iowa and Manchester Metropolitan University. He is now Professor of Poetry at Sheffield University.

Question: Teaching is very different from your other activities. What do you get out of it?

Answer: Community (writing means being on your own) and dialogue. Challenge, too: challenging my students, and being challenged by them. It's a stimulus to thought, a renewal if you like, and it underlines for me the importance of having someone to guide you, in the way that I was by Peter Sansom, when I attended his writing workshops at Huddersfield Polytechnic in the eighties.

> Simon has won many awards for his work, from the *Sunday Times* Young Author of the Year Poetry Prize in 1992 to a CBE for services to poetry in 2010.

Question: What do awards mean to you?

Answer: A kind of validation, maybe, by implying that people are reading my work? I think of myself as a communicator, so it's important to me that someone is listening, otherwise I'm just talking to myself.

Simon Armitage is now one of the most widely studied and taught poets in the country, and features in the English Literature specifications of all the major examining bodies

Question: Are you pleased that your poems are studied by school students? Were you interested in poetry at school?

Answer: I never write poems with the idea that they might be studied; it's just a happy coincidence if they are useful in an educational context. But I got interested in poetry when I was at school, so it's an opportunity for my poems to catch someone's eye in the same way, or to whisper in their ear or turn their head. I like the idea that there's a kid like me out there somewhere, daydreaming his life away, interested in nothing, going nowhere, then suddenly a poem turns a switch on in his head. I'd be happy to be the author of that poem.

Question: There often seems to be an adult perception that kids no longer enjoy poetry. Do you think that's true?

Answer: It's true that poetry is never going to be for everybody. It's not a mainstream art form, and requires concentration, and has to compete in a very crowded marketplace. But I see poetry doing very well at festivals and events, and the extraordinary success of Poetry Live! speaks volumes. As many as 2,000 school students at a time gathering to listen to poetry for four hours – it shouldn't work, according to the pessimists, but it absolutely does. People are still interested in one individual saying something they've truly thought about and saying it in a measured and memorable way. I can't imagine that will ever change.

Sample Student Essays

Below are three sample essays written in response to GCSE exam questions. Each one is followed by a commentary, explaining what grade the essay might have achieved in the exam, and why. Although two are based on the AQA Anthology and one on the Edexcel Anthology, the skills the students show would place them in these bands in either specification.

Essay One: Compare the ways relationship between the speaker and another person are presented in 'Give' and 'The River God'.

The speakers in 'Give' and 'The River God' are in very different situations. The river god is in control of the other character in the poem, but in 'Give' the person the beggar is addressing is in control, because they can choose whether to give the beggar some money or not.

The river god initially seems to be benevolent, as 'where my fish float by I bless their swimming', and he likes 'the people to bathe in me'. It is soon clear that he has a much darker side, though. 'Especially women' sounds a bit creepy, and when he says that he throws drowning people up 'in a spirit of clowning' you can see how nasty he really is, to enjoy taking people's lives. In the second half of the poem his perverted nature really appears, when you realise that there is a body trapped underwater in the reeds, and that the river god sees her as his 'beautiful dear'. The relationship in 'Give' is not like this, as both the characters are still alive, unlike in 'The River God' and neither holds the power of life and death over the other, although the beggar's life seems pretty miserable, and the other person could help if he or she wanted to. The river god definitely does not want to help anybody, unless it's helping them to drown.

There is some threat in 'Give', though, but it's not as dangerous as the threats of the river god, who can 'drown the fools/who bathe too close to the weir, contrary to rules'. The beggar's threat is just an emotional one, not a physical one. He seems to have deliberately set out to embarrass the woman he's begging from by choosing 'here' to make a scene, and 'yours' is the doorway where he's chosen to sleep. He repeats 'of all the . . .' to make you think it's deliberate. At the end the line 'You give me tea. That's big of you' doesn't sound sincere. The beggar wants more, even if it's 'just change'.

The poems are written quite differently. 'The River God' has lots of flow, just like a river does, with lots of long sentences and enjambment. 'Give' has much shorter sentences, which make you think he's desperate.

Examiner Commentary

The second paragraph is a response to the character of the river god, supported, then explained, then **sustained**, and the fourth paragraph shows the same skill in dealing with 'Give'. The essay begins with a comparative comment, and then the third paragraph shows some structured comments on similarities and differences. By the time the candidate writes 'the beggar's threat is an emotional one, not a physical one' this has **become sustained focus on comparison**. There is clearly some **understanding** of the beggar's attitude to the other person.

These three qualities all indicate a candidate operating in the C range. There is a weakness, however, as Assessment Objective 2, which deals with the effects of writer's methods, is not dealt with very well. The first time it is addressed is in the sentence 'He repeats . . .' in the fourth paragraph, where an effect is identified, not explained. The last paragraph appears to address methods more directly, but again the effects of 'flow' and 'make you think he's desperate' are only identified. The whole response would sit in the C band, but not at the top, because of this weakness.

Essay Two: Compare the ways feelings are presented in 'Out of the Blue' and 'Bayonet Charge'.

The openings of the poems demonstrate the difference of the two characters' situations and feelings. The speaker in 'Out of the Blue' is static, unable to move, and the sentences are short: the first line is end-stopped, as though the speaker is trapped in a short space. There are five sentences in the first eight lines, whereas the first sentence in 'Bayonet Charge' races across ten lines as the soldier 'awoke and was running'. Hughes drives the sentence forward with punctuation, as three of the lines end in a dash, which automatically makes the reader pick up again quickly at the beginning of the next line. The first line starts with 'suddenly', as though the poem starts in the middle of an event. There is a dash before the last word, and then an enjambment, taking the line quickly into the next.

The soldier here is running in fear, but the speaker in 'Out of the Blue' is trapped in fear and repeats words and word forms constantly, as though unable to move away, with the same fact beating at him all the time. No fewer than 37 words in the poem end in 'ing', which might normally suggest movement, but here usually implies stasis. The three words repeated exactly are 'waving', as the man stands helplessly signalling, 'watching', and 'appalling', which is the man's response to the one movement he does not want to make, the fall from the tower. This feeling is emphasised by the full stop between the words and then the line break ('Appalling. Appalling'), so that the reader is forced to linger over the word. No words are repeated next to each other like this in 'Bayonet Charge', though the word 'running' is repeated three times, the last one being 'still running', this being a poem of swift action. Four action words are put together in 'Out of the Blue', but again they are describing the swift action that the speaker dreads: 'wind-milling, wheeling, spiralling, falling'. The question marks in the poems have different effects, too. There are three in quick succession in 'Out of the Blue', suggesting the man's desperation as he appeals to the watchers to see 'a soul worth saving'. The simple, desperate plea 'So when will you come?' is made sharper by being in monosyllables, in a line on its own. The one question mark in 'Bayonet Charge' is buried in the middle of a line, and expresses 'bewilderment' about his situation rather than panic, at that moment anyway.

Both poems use personification to make objects seem dangerous. In 'Out of the Blue' the heat is 'bullying, driving' the man towards the edge. In 'Bayonet Charge' the heat of the explosion is presented as 'a yellow hare' (suggesting speed of movement again) that 'rolled' and 'crawled', and is made more horrifying and predatory with the vivid descriptions of the hare's mouth and eyes.

The endings of the poems are very different. 'Bayonet Charge' ends explosively, with 'blue crackling air' and 'touchy dynamite', and noisily – 'a yelling alarm'. By contrast, the ending of 'Out of the Blue' seems slow, with two end-stopped lines, the lack of feeling in 'numb', and the downbeat final couplet of 'sagging' and 'flag-ging'. There is a sense of imminent defeat here, and the certainty of death, whereas in 'Bayonet Charge' the soldier still has a chance 'to get out of' the situation. Both men are desperate to escape, but the history of the attack on the twin towers tells us that one, at least, is doomed.

Examiner Commentary

This is an **analytical** response to the task from the beginning. The student here structures her response around differences in presenta-tion, which the task asks for, not differences in feelings , and this enables her to explore different methods. **Analysis of the writers' methods** is shown in the first paragraph when dealing with the openings of the poems, and this skill is shown again several times. Although some of the comparative comments are just links, the comparison develops through the response, and the final paragraph shows **analytical comparison.**

This response clearly belongs in the A band. Perhaps the student concentrated too much on techniques in the end, so that meanings were not really explored. This might prevent a mark at the top of A, though flashes of close analysis might compensate for this. For A* the student does not really evaluate the effects she has analysed, though, or examined very closely one moment or feature of the poems. To see a student doing this, read the final response below. Even if the student is writing about poems you have not studied, you should be able to identify the skills of **close analysis** and **evaluation** used in the response.

Essay Three: Compare how 'Those bastards in their mansions' and 'The Penelopes of my homeland' present oppression. (Edexcel)

'Those bastards in their mansions' and 'The Penelopes of my homeland' both present the victims of oppression, but in very different ways. The attitudes to oppression seem very different. In 'The Penelopes' the women seem passive, and helpless in the face of their ignorance of their husbands' fate. Their lives and their dreams are over, 'without realising, without ever thinking'. In 'Those bastards' the oppression is more physical than mental: 'cuffs and shackles' and iron on their 'wrists and ankles'. They must be actively aware of what is happening, or, in the speaker's case, likely to happen. With the Penelopes, what has happened is in the past, and they are waiting in vain, not for more oppression but for the restoration of their men. They are defeated by their oppression, as they

> died slowly
> carrying their dreams to their graves

and the poem ends with the view that another cycle of oppression
is beginning:

> leaving more Penelopes to take their place.

In 'Those bastards' the possibility of escape from oppression and
tyranny seems very real, as the speaker has

> told the people how to ditch their cuffs and shackles

and seems ready to fight (unlike the Penelopes), though not yet: 'I
stick to the shadows'.

In the Prometheus myth that underlies 'Those bastards' the cycle
of oppression was real, and physical, as Prometheus was 'picked at
by their eagles' every day. Armitage has altered this myth, or at least
its time frame, as the speaker is aware of this possibility, but it hasn't
happened to him yet. Hardi also alters the myth but to different ef-
fect: these Penelopes, waiting patiently for the return of their Odys-
seuses, will simply grow 'old and older', 'without ever knowing that
they should stop waiting', because unlike the mythical Odysseus their
husbands will never return. The outcome of 'Those bastards' could be
seen as uplifting, as the hero is still functioning, and could rise against
his oppressors; 'The Penelopes' has the opposite effect, as hope is
absent. This is all the more affecting for being a real situation: unlike
Armitage's re-imagining of the Prometheus myth, these Penelopes
are real, as the epigraph 'for the 50,000 widows of Anfal' shows.

The stories are presented very differently. The writing of 'The
Penelopes' is deceptively simple. Each of the first five stanzas begins
'Years and years', the simple repetition underlining the length of
the wait, and echoed within each stanza by repetitions of words and
phrases, so that the poem takes on an incantatory feel. Each stanza

subtly deals with a different aspect of their wait, but the final stanza, shorn of the 'years and years' refrain, reads like an epitaph, with the title reprised in the line

> The Penelopes of my homeland died slowly.

The Armitage poem is much more obviously devised, with the hard sounds which characterise the poem kicked off by 'Those bastards', and the verbs placed at the beginning and end of lines capturing the action and aggression of the piece, quite unlike the quiet patience of Penelope: 'vaulted', 'crossed', 'forced', 'lifted'. The poem echoes throughout, sometimes obviously ('shackles' and 'ankles') and sometimes less so ('beagles' and 'grilled'.)

The poem is one of many in which Armitage plays with sonnet form. There are four irregular stanzas, and no clear rhyme scheme, but this enables Armitage to shape a highly effective ending. The thirteenth line, 'beneath the sun' is the shortest in the poem, exaggerating the gap to the last line, and heightening its drama:

> Me, I stick to the shadows, carry a gun.

Like Hardi's three-line ending, this sums up the poem, in a way, or at least the speaker's situation and attitude, the finality helped by the gap before it and the fact that it is an end-stopped single sentence line. 'Me' as the first word, accentuated further by the pause the comma makes after it, adds to the sense of a definition of the character. The full rhyme at the end, only the second in the poem, falls on the word 'gun', suggesting that the figure lurking 'in the shadows' is perhaps ready to attack, not just defend, in armed conflict.

'The Penelopes of my homeland' also ends with a rhyme, or at least an assonance, for the first time in the poem. 'Graves' and 'place', though, are in another world from the short, aggressive sound and meaning of 'gun'. This rounds off an elegy, not only for the dead husbands and the dead Penelopes, but also for the Penelopes to

come, who will 'take their place'. Armitage's ending may be uplift-
ing for the reader, or even inspiring, but the chilling lament for the
Penelopes whose husbands were or will be the victims of genocide is
surely more moving, even though it seems simply stated.

Examiner Commentary

This response is closely comparative from the beginning, **exploring
the differences** in attitudes to oppression, and exploring and analys-
ing meanings. The end of the paragraph referring to the widows of
Anfal achieves **evaluative comparison.** The paragraph around the last
line of 'Those bastards' shows **close analysis of detail** and **convincing
interpretation,** and the final paragraph is again highly **evaluative.** It
is a **perceptive and convincing** response. **A full-mark essay.**

Essay Four: How does Armitage make 'Mother any distance
greater than a single span' particularly interesting for you?

Any teenage reader is likely to be interested by this poem, as it exam-
ines a moment when a young man breaks free from the confines of
home into the excitement and uncertainties of independent adult life.

   The poem begins with mother and son working closely together:
she is a 'second pair of hands' for the young man, and the first two
stanzas see 'you' and 'me' working in tandem. They are still joined to-
gether, by the 'line' of the measuring tape, which the reader inevitably
sees as the umbilical cord as it is 'still feeding out', a vital and life-
giving connection. At the same time, though, it is unreeling 'years
between us' which suggests both their closeness through time and
the increasing distance, in lines full of the language of measurement.

   The poem reaches its breaking point right in the middle, inter-
estingly, with the two words 'Anchor. Kite.' This is the fulcrum of
the poem: the first word after the break caused by the new stanza is

'I', and it is the speaker's progress which dominates the rest of the poem, as he 'space-walks' up the ladder, an image neatly combining the idea of somebody still attached to a mother ship, but in the freedom of the sky, 'an endless sky' which 'opens' in front of him as he reaches for the 'hatch' – an appropriate word, combining the space imagery with the idea of a bird hatching, a bird that will soon 'fly the nest' – or perhaps not.

'Anchor. Kite' leaps off the page for the reader in an interesting way. The sharp 'k' sounds and the single-word sentences are arresting after the sentence full of long 'e' sounds which flows over several lines, and the stanza break after 'kite' further lifts out the words. The anchor comes first, as the mother did, still in control, and either supporting or holding back the son, depending on how you view it. Many teenage boys would think it was the latter, but the speaker here merely offers the contrast without judgement. He continues to climb away, though, and knows that 'something has to give'. The mother is pictured holding on desperately, perfectly captured in the rhyme of 'pinch' and 'inch' followed by the ellipses, the three dots seeming to represent the last drops of contact. The use of punctuation to affect the reader's response in this way, both here and in the full stops in 'Anchor. Kite.' which divide and join the mother and son, is one of the most interesting features of the writing here.

The whole poem works up to the breaking point between the two, but the outcome is uncertain. As much as the boy wants to 'fly', he knows that he might 'fall' also in the face of the perils of independence. Again, Armitage cunningly suggests the gap of the unknown before the son through manipulating form and structure. The poem does not end neatly with the completion of the fourteenth line of a sonnet, but continues with four more words, 'to fall or fly', perfectly balanced (as on the edge of the nest, perhaps) but with a gap in front of them, as glancing at the page shows.

It's particularly interesting that Armitage does not go for the simple 'fly' at the end, which might be imagined to appeal to the young male reader, but instead is cautious and balancing to the end, aware of the dangers. Instinct makes the mother want to hold on to her son; but it's instinct also that the son will launch himself into life without her, whatever his fears might be.

Examiner Commentary

This response is a full-mark essay. It offers a sophisticated interpretation of the text, but also shows awareness of other interpretations, as in the fourth paragraph. Detail is evaluated precisely at the end of the third paragraph, around the word 'hatch', and sensitive understanding of the effects of the writer's choices of language, structure and form is shown in dealing with 'Anchor. Kite.' and the effects of the last four words of the poem. The student touches on a number of details in the poem, but by no means all; that would be unnecessary, as the student shows the skills of understanding required to achieve full marks by examining closely and perceptively those details that are addressed.

Further Reading

Websites

simonarmitage.com
faber.co.uk
bbc.co.uk/schools/gcsebitesize/english_literature/poetarmitage
bbc.co.uk/learningzone/clips/SimonArmitageWritingPoems
poetryarchive.org
britishcouncil.org

Works by Simon Armitage
(published by Faber and Faber unless otherwise stated)

poetry

Zoom! (Bloodaxe Books)
Xanadu (Bloodaxe Books)
Kid
Book of Matches
The Dead Sea Poems
Moon Country (with Glyn Maxwell)
CloudCuckooLand
Killing Time
Selected Poems
Travelling Songs
The Universal Home Doctor
Tyrannosaurus Rex Versus the Corduroy Kid
The Not Dead (Pomona Books)
Out of the Blue (Enitharmon)
Seeing Stars

drama

Eclipse
Mister Heracles (after Euripides)
Jerusalem
Black Roses: The Killing of Sophie Lancaster (Enitharmon)

prose

All Points North (Penguin)
Little Green Man (Penguin
The White Stuff (Penguin)
Gig: The Life and Times of a Rock-Star Fantasist (Penguin)
Walking Home: Travels with a Troubadour on the Pennine Way

translation

Homer's Odyssey
Sir Gawain and the Green Knight
The Death of King Arthur

The GCSE poems

'About His Person' (from *Kid*)
'Alaska' (from *Kid*)
'Gooseberry Season' (from *Kid*)
'In Our Tenth Year' (from *Kid*)
'Kid' (from *Kid*)
'Mice and snakes don't give me the shivers' (from *Book of Matches*)
'Mother, any distance greater than a single span' (from *Book of Matches*)
'My father thought it bloody queer' (from *Book of Matches*)
'Poem' (from *Zoom!*)
'The Convergence of the Twain' (from *Travelling Songs*)
'To Poverty' (from *Book of Matches*)
'True North' (from *Kid*)
'Wintering Out' (from *Kid*)
'Without Photographs' (from *Kid*)
'The Clown Punk' (from *Tyannosaurus Rex Versus the Corduroy Kid*)
'Give' (from *The Dead Sea Poems*)
'A Vision' (from *Tyannosaurus Rex Versus the Corduroy Kid*)
'Extract from Out of the Blue' (from *Out of the Blue*)
'The Manhunt' (from *The Not Dead*)
'Harmonium' (unpublished)
'Hitcher' (from *Book of Matches*)
'Those Bastards in their Mansions' (from *Book of Matches*)